SOME MODERN AMERICAN POETS

Some Modern American Poets

By James G. Southworth

*M.A. (Oxon), Ph.D. (Harv.); Professor of English, University of
Toledo (Ohio), U.S.A.*

Author of *Sowing the Spring; Studies in British Poets from Hopkins
to MacNeice; The Poetry of Thomas Hardy; Vauxhall Gardens*

BASIL BLACKWELL
OXFORD
1950

Printed in Great Britain for THE SHAKESPEARE HEAD PRESS
by A. R. MOWBRAY & CO. LIMITED, London and Oxford
and published by BASIL BLACKWELL & MOTT LTD.

CONTENTS

PREFACE

THE present collection of essays, intended for the general reader and not for the scholar, should in no way be understood to attempt a history of modern American poetry. Were this its aim, certain poets included might have been neglected and certain poets not included must have been considered. Mr. Sandburg and Masters, for example, for their extension of Whitman's prosody and for broadening the scope of Whitman's subject-matter; Lindsay for his innovations; Mr. Ezra Pound for his profound influence on the *avant garde* group of the early twenties, and others. Mr. Pound's importance, however, is more than historical. Neither have I attempted to indicate the place of any one of the included poets in that history. What I have attempted is to appraise the work of each as absolute poetry according to the tenets of classical criticism. My approach has been an aesthetic one. The basis of judgment rests on years of close association with the acknowledged great poets as well as those under discussion. In order that my opinion may be that of the present rather than a carry-over from years when my sense of taste was less than I hope it is to-day, I have reread the work of those poets included in the present volume. As Walpole remarked, the reader 'has to see that he is perpetually at work at developing his sense of taste and touch of vision.'

Many will wonder at the omission of Mr. T. S. Eliot or of Mr. W. H. Auden, now an American citizen. The reason is an obvious one. I have written on both in *Sowing the Spring*, a volume of essays on the modern British poets, now out of print.

The arrangement of the essays is strictly chronological. I think the reader will do wisely not to read them in the order as they appear, but as his interest moves him. It will be abundantly clear from the *Introduction* that in my opinion

Mr. Frost is the only modern American poet with sufficient stature to take his place among the great poets. I am strongly tempted to say that he is the greatest poet America has yet produced.

The reader who is looking for a thesis will look in vain. I have had no axe to grind and have tried to be as objective as possible. I hope, too, that neither congeniality nor lack of congeniality to the subject-matter has obscured my sense of the true value of the poetry as such. It is natural to suppose, however, that in two poets of equal ability in expression and profundity of thought, the one whose thought is more congenial with my own will unconsciously be preferred to another with whom I am intellectually at variance. Each poet seems, too, to call for a difference of treatment.

My indebtednesses are many and I should like to acknowledge them at the present. My greatest debt will always be to the late Dr. A. J. Carlyle, who not only insisted that I stand on my own feet critically but constantly stressed the fact that no generation can accept the critical evaluations of a preceding one. To do so spells the death of criticism. To others, my debt is more specific. To Dr. Ernest Gray for his careful reading and criticism of the manuscript, most of whose suggestions have been accepted and incorporated in the present text; to Mr. Martin Scholten and Miss Ruby Scott for help on many specific problems; and to Mr. Norman Ault for his invaluable help in detecting Americanisms that would be unfamiliar to the English reader. A different debt is owed to Mrs. Dudley Waters of Grand Rapids, Michigan. In her dedication of herself to a life of service to her country, its people, and her own high ideals, she represents the American aristocratic tradition at its finest. She has been a constant inspiration to all who have enjoyed the privilege of her friendship.

Toledo, Ohio, U.S.A.
September 15, 1949.

INTRODUCTION

GENERALIZATIONS about American poets and American poetry can never be of greater validity than as a starting point for a discussion which must descend the ladder of abstraction to a consideration of the characteristics of each poet. The present chapter is such a starting point. The essays on the individual poets following are still largely abstractions, and because they are, must be read as one person's opinion. Mr. Stevens has aptly expressed the reason for such an attitude. To be real, he says, each must 'find for himself his earth, his sky, his sea' ('Holiday in Reality'). If we hope to do this, we must also remember with Mr. Frost that

> We were not given eyes or intellect
> For all the light at once the source of light—
> For wisdom that can have no counterwisdom.
> *The Masque of Mercy*

In spite of superficial resemblances in American culture, particularly of the populace, we must remember that America lacks homogeneity. The greater diversity among us than among the English, French, Germans, Italians, and others, of racial, emotional, economic, and educational factors, will elicit a greater diversity of responses from American poets than would be evident in the work of the same number of English poets. Nor must we overlook the environmental factors of geography. It would be idle to expect the same point of view toward all except the ultimate necessities of life from the New Englander, particularly those north of Boston, the Middle-Westerner, the Southerner, the Texan, Californian, or North-Westerner. Mr. MacLeish has given excellent expression to the unfortunate result of the lack of homogeneity in his 'American Letter.'

The time factor is equally important. Some of our poets had their roots firmly planted before the first World War; others finding themselves almost rootless in the post-war period, found it difficult or impossible to send their roots deep; still another group has arrived at maturity during the second World War and since. But in spite of these divergent factors, more clearly than at any other time in our history can it be said that we can hear America singing or trying to sing, and that the poets are trying to sing songs of themselves as well as the songs of the country. We should err greatly, however, in thinking that their voices are uniformly good or that as 'makers' they have had, one and all, the talent, patience, self-discipline, and vision to have created timeless songs.

After fifteen years of constant association with the work of those whose admirers have been most vocal, I have reluctantly been forced to the conclusion that they sang for the moment and that their chance of survival is negligible. The work of many, like that of Masters, Lindsay, and Mr. Sandburg, may possess sociological or historical value in that they not only broadened the scope of subject-matter, but helped to strike off the prosodic shackles which prevented the finding or the using of the proper idiom for the thoughts and spirit peculiar to America. A few of their individual poems will merit a permanent place in any anthology of American poetry. Robinson, a greater artist than these three, is particularly effective in many of his shorter poems, although I am unable to share the enthusiasm of his admirers for his longer works. His prepossession has been with the earth rather than the sky, with the failures rather than with those who can stalwartly face the fact that 'The saddest thing in life Is that the best thing in it should be courage.' This quality of negation in his work will eventually militate against him. But more than his subject-matter, it is his polysyllabic diction that tires me. He sometimes uses this diction effectively, as in 'Flammonde,' to communicate his protagonist's graciousness, but he also employs it otherwise until it begins to pall. He is at his best in his sonnets where the limitations of the form curb his prolixity.

In spite of the obvious differences in the poets included in the present volume, certain basic aims are evident. Mr. Eliot has stressed the necessity for finding rhythms for poetry that reflect modern speech rhythms. This accepted 'must' for poets—it has, of course, always been a characteristic of the great tradition of poetry since Chaucer—every modern poet of any value whatever has attempted to solve for himself in his own way. It is a tenet, however, that needs constant restatement. Whether each has succeeded or not the reader must finally decide for himself, although it is obvious that there are almost as many different concepts of what that speech-rhythm is as there are poets. Mr. Eliot has found it in varying degrees and in varying periods of his poetic life in James Joyce's *Ulysses* (particularly the Stephen Daedalus sections), the Elizabethan dramatists, Lancelot Andrewes, and the English Church ritual. Mr. Frost has found it in the folk-speech of New England—has taken it from the soil itself. His verse has the relaxation of a Greek statue; the careful reader is always aware of the strength of the unflexed muscles. Emily Dickinson has caught the speech-rhythm of intense feminine exhilaration and excitement; Mr. Stevens from the application of an incisive intellect in the efficient manner of business—its tone is brittle and stenographic; and Mr. Mac-Leish in his later propagandist poems from the pseudo-speech rhythms of radio 'soap' opera.[1] Others have found it in other ways and in all of them it is manifested in a directness of statement. Too often, however, in trying to be terse they end by being obscure in spite of syntactical regularities.

Another reason for obscurity in modern poetry is the attempt by some poets to save their verses from prosiness by their search for the unusual word, or by giving the usual word

[1] Soap-opera: a radio drama, presented serially over long periods, usually sponsored by a soap manufacturer.

an unaccustomed meaning. The vocabulary of Mr. Frost and Emily Dickinson is generally simple. Mr. Frost is content with the word's generally accepted meaning; but Miss Dickinson often renders passages obscure by using familiar words with a distinctly private and personal connotation that baffles the reader. Following the example of Mr. Stevens, Hart Crane ransacked literature and the dictionary for the unusual word. This practice has received added impetus from Mr. Auden, who has not only rifled the section of Webster's *New International Dictionary* in pearl type—'mornes of motted mamelons,' 'sopronon,' and others—but has used words not even to be found there.[1] This tendency is particularly pronounced in younger men like Messrs. Shapiro, Lowell, and Jarrell, although frequent, too, in Robinson. Tradition supports them, however, and the practice is commendable when used for greater sharpness of impact, or to restore 'such good and natural English words as have been long time out of use and almost clean disinherited.' Nevertheless, the reader must frequently wish a more familiar word had been employed when the familiar one would be equally, or more, effective. In the work of several of the younger poets the self-conscious use of the esoteric word destroys the intrinsic form by faulty emphasis. Mr. Stevens also expects from his *élite* reader a knowledge of French. Instead of impressing the reader, however, who has such a knowledge, the poet's use of French strikes him as pure affectation. The poets would do well to remember Horace's statement that they will have expressed themselves 'admirably if a clever setting gives a spice of novelty to a familiar word,' and to heed Longinus' warning that by trying too hard for something unusual and original, they are apt, instead, to achieve frigidity and puerility.

When this search rises from the desire for accurate connotation, the practice is justifiable. Too many of our words have

[1] Webster's *New International*, a standard American unabridged dictionary, places the unusual words at the foot of the page in type smaller than the rest.

admittedly lost their freshness because of their vulgar use, and the poet is to be commended who is artist enough to take the path of greatest resistance. He is under no compulsion to cater for the easy reader. When, however, he does it to call attention to himself rather than to the communication of the poem this tendency is deplorable, just as is any technical swagger. Too often, I am afraid, a young poet strives for obscurity because of the poverty, or imperfect crystallization, of his thought. He mistakes obscurity for profundity.

The texture of poetry is largely determined by the poet's power to achieve his magic by his arrangement or grouping of words. It is by this faculty that he largely evokes the basic emotion associated with his thought. Of the poets in the present volume Mr. Frost, Emily Dickinson, and Hart Crane are pre-eminent in this respect. It is this ability to suffuse their thought with emotion that gives lasting vitality to their work and brings the reader to it again and again. Mr. Cummings and Mr. MacLeish both do this in occasional lyrics, but the occasions are limited. Were pure verbal harmonies the ultimate desideratum, Mr. Conrad Aiken, one of America's most felicitously musical poets, would rank higher than he does; but he has too often sacrificed strength for music, and the reader eventually tires of the treatment. It has too much the effect of music by Tschaikowsky and Strauss rather than that by Mozart, Schubert, Bach, or Beethoven. In other words, it is irresistible during one period of our emotional growth, but it is a period we soon outgrow. When we return to him it is to such poems as 'The Road' and 'Tetélestai,' and even these begin to impress us with a sense of over-ripeness or decadence. One misses a sinewy quality.

Nowhere do the poets reveal their consciousness of the American scene, however, as they do in their images. Here one finds freshness and the exploration of divers areas of experience. A poet's images often, of course, reveal more about him than do any consciously stated biographical facts.

Emily Dickinson's, for example, are largely drawn from sewing, cookery, and the garden. She illuminates the realms of the absolute with these domestic images in a startling way. Mr. Frost's are broader in scope and reveal his closeness to the earth and the manifold contacts with all kinds of society. Their homeliness should not blind the reader to their intellectuality. Nowhere are Mr. Frost and Miss Dickinson so much New Englanders as in their images. Mr. Jeffers has given a distinctive quality to his verse by his use of the California coast for his images; Mr. MacLeish by his early use of the Middle-West for his; and Mr. Benét of New York for his. Hart Crane in seeking the ultimate of sensation paid too dear a price for several of his, excellent though they be.

The degrees of muscularity in these images varies from the easy ones of Benét, the vague ones of Jeffers, to the sharply focused ones of Crane and Stevens. Just as Aiken may make an entire poem out of a sustained simile ('Portrait of a Girl'), so Stevens makes a series of poems out of metaphors. One of the reasons for Stevens' rather limited following is his consistent use of highly wrought metaphor.[1]

The diversity of unaccustomed symbols in modern poetry demands constant alertness from its readers. Lacking the imagination capable of an occasional extensive leap, the reader falls into the slough of misunderstanding. Mr. Frost demands less spectacular feats from his reader, but he is not the naïve person the unwary is apt to think him. His casual and relaxed manner is disarming; but the reader who under-estimates his lithe, sinewy mind will miss much in his work that merits the closest attention. He appears casual only because he is a great artist.

It is needless to repeat here the influences of older poets on the modern. Perhaps never before have the poets of one

---

[1] Unless I err because of close association with his work, the reader unacquainted with him would probably do well to begin with his latest book, *Transport to Summer*. Here the metaphor is more easily grasped than in the relatively early *The Man With The Blue Guitar*.

generation pillaged the past as those of the present have done. Some have attempted to sever their connection with the great tradition. When they broke too completely, they failed. It is a heartening sign to see the willingness of younger poets to work from within that tradition rather than to attack it from without. Only by such means does the great tradition constantly renew and alter itself. Attack from without enrages only those attacking; it makes no impression on the *original* poets of the period being subjected to attack. Attack from within soon reveals the drones who have willingly accepted the work of others and have made no contribution of their own. Mr. Frost has poked gentle fun at those who have been too esoteric in their borrowings.

The reader of modern poetry must not expect to find its influences confined only to poets, any more than the poets of any generation have taken all their ideas from preceding poets. To think this is to misunderstand the poet. From the point of view of their ideas, many moderns are working in the tradition of the nineteenth-century novelists, and are keenly aware of the alterations in thought about the universe resulting from the discoveries of science. Their social consciousness has been quickened. Mr. Frost has the broadest base of reading of any American poet. He is in many ways the most truly intellectual, but he wears his learning with a lightness that misleads many. He not only reveals a large and comprehensive grasp of the poets working in the great tradition from the Greek and Hebrew to the present day, but he has more completely assimilated than any other poet the scientific discoveries down to and including those of Einstein, himself a poet in the extensiveness of his imagination. To understand the forces behind modern American poetry one must be familiar with many of our colonial writers, with Melville, Emerson, Thoreau, and Whitman; with Shakespeare, Jonson, Webster, Ford, and other Elizabethans; with Herrick, Vaughan, and Herbert; with the eighteenth-century satirists

B

and Blake; with Wordsworth, Keats, Shelley, the Brownings, Ruskin; with the Bible, St. Thomas, Dante; with Huxley, Darwin, and Einstein; with Werner Jaeger's *Paideia* and the great Greek and Latin classics; with Baudelaire, Rimbaud, and LaForgue, to name but a few of the most important. It would be futile to attempt to trace these many influences on the several modern poets. It is enough to know that these influences are at work.

As interesting, however, as are any of the technical achievements, or influences on modern poets, are the poets' attitudes towards life and their adjustment thereto, particularly to many of the so-called imponderables. It is natural that a young poet should be concerned with the problem of self-integration in the welter of complex forces that are shaping contemporary civilization. This struggle and his gradually increasing consciousness of the realities of life furnish him his subject-matter. As his emotional nature expands under some of the stimuli, he is likely to lose himself in a life of the emotions and strive to experience the heights and depths of feeling. This may lead the emotionally immature to take what Mr. Frost has aptly called the position of 'straddling' with one foot in the clouds, the other in the gutter. Hart Crane is one of the most regrettable examples of this. Having rightly rejected the life of negation such as was being expressed by Mr. Eliot in *The Waste Land*, he sought to find the synthesis of life otherwise than by the means of most arduous endeavour in his personal affairs. He too early ceased struggling and ruined himself by his dissipations.

Other young idealists have been outraged by what they have been confronted with, and have poured out their disgust in poems which may be sharply focused but are distorted because of an unfortunate angle of vision. Such are some of Mr. Cummings' 'realistic' poems. But not all the younger poets of the early twenties were maladjusted. Although readers may disagree about the relative merits of Mr. MacLeish

and Stephen Vincent Benét, no one would look upon them as
not having attained emotional as well as intellectual maturity.
The most persistent product of an idealism which, once outraged, has been incapable of achieving emotional maturity is
the work of Mr. Robinson Jeffers.

Fortunately, the young poets of to-day—Shapiro, Lowell,
Jarrell, Horan, and others—are not in the same position as
the young men of the early twenties. They went into war
with their eyes open and they matured during the war years.
Their work is affirmative in that they have had the ability
and courage resolutely to face facts. Eventually, if they are
able to develop a greater technical ability, their growth as
artists will be significant for poetry. We must not neglect
the influence on this note of affirmation of that group of
English poets—Auden, Spender, Day Lewis, and MacNeice—
whose impact on our younger poets was felt before the last
war.

Love as a theme for poetry is, of course, as inevitable as it is
natural. Modern poetry, however, has extended the range of
love poetry in opposite directions. To my knowledge no one
has ever given such full, complete, and profound expression
to married love as has Mr. Frost. I am speaking of married
love from the man's point of view. The person who has not
glimpsed what Mr. Frost is writing about in these poems of
complete fulfilment may object to the seeming lack of passion;
but no other modern approaches him in the communication
of a profound passion devoid of gross sensuality, but not of
sensuousness. Some readers will prefer the ecstatic outpourings of love by Emily Dickinson. Nowhere is she more
sentimental, more the frustrated, terrified person than in her
poems on love. It is easier for her to face the doubts about
God than the realities of love. Mr. Aiken and Mr. Cummings
have written love poems of rare and compelling beauty.
Mr. Cummings, however, has failed to mature in his attitude

toward love. At fifty he is still writing poems acceptable
from a poet of twenty, but not from a man of that age.

The opposite extension of the range of love is the treatment
of homosexual love. Poets like Mr. Spender, Mr. Auden,
and Hart Crane have expressed themselves frankly; others less
overtly. Since Proust it has become the theme of many novels,
most of them poor. Although there is no basic reason for
its suppression as a subject, there remain certain practical ones
which may in time be overcome by the followers of the
pioneers—but only may. The fact that society regards homo-
sexuality as it does makes it almost impossible for the artist
to be completely sincere in his treatment of it. He cannot be
sufficiently objective. Possibly because of a guilt complex,
conscious or sub-conscious, he gives to his treatment a wrong
emphasis. He is either blatant or unduly sentimental. Until
as artist he can rid himself of the prepossessions that distort
his vision, he should leave it alone. Hart Crane was able so to
shape it as poetic material. So, too, have been Mr. Spender,
in some of his shorter lyrics and *Vienna*, and Mr. Auden.
But the majority of poets as well as novelists have failed
lamentably. The notes of self-justification, apology, or moral
condemnation are rarely absent. From the point of view of the
general reader, too great an ignorance of the subject still
persists for him to be able to understand the nuances of the
poet. He cannot avoid the intrusion of what Mr. Richards
aptly calls 'mnemonic irrelevance.'

The reader seeking guidance for his political views will find
all degrees of thinking from the extreme left to the moderate
and extreme right. He will find ardent 'new-dealers,' middle-
roaders, and strong conservatives; he will find champions of
the proletariat and champions of the economic-royalists. Not
unaccountably, he will find the arc from left through moderate
to right paralleling the age of the poet, and the degree of his
possession of a sense of humour. The following essays will,

I trust, correct some of the errors of sweeping generalizations about the Marxist content of modern poetry.

The fundamentalist in religion will find himself shocked by the religious attitude of many modern poets, almost as frightened as some of the poets have found themselves when confronted by their own inability to reconcile fact with wish. Several of the young poets have followed Mr. Eliot's lead and turned toward Anglo-Catholicism; some toward Rome. Others, like Mr. Jeffers, have made a religion of pain. To me the most mature poets in their religious attitudes are Mr. Frost and Mr. Stevens. Each has strenuously sought the absolutes. In most ways no two poets could be more unlike than they, but in this relentless search they are the same. Because Mr. Frost has gone as far as he has in *The Masque of Mercy*, critics have found him less satisfactory than heretofore. From my own point of view, however, and because I am Protestant enough not to be able to accept a religion of external authority, he has taken the only satisfactory direction. Instead of a falling off, I see the resignation that comes from complete humility and acceptance—the same point at which Milton had arrived in *Samson Agonistes*. The faith still possible in the seventeenth century is, of course, no longer tenable since the discoveries of Einstein. But as Frost has recognized, the scientific truths of Genesis have been superseded, but not the great moral truths. Many of our younger poets have been unable to realize that with the passage of the scientific truth of the Bible and the great books of the past, their moral truths remain. It is strange that Emily Dickinson, circumscribed as her life was in all but the range of her intellect, saw what many of the younger moderns have been unable to see. With her these moments of wisdom alternated with moments of wishful thinking when she shrank from the arduous and strenuous task of facing new and startling revelations.

Closely linked to the attitude of the modern poets toward religion is their attitude toward pain. The word has been used so repeatedly to cover every degree of experience from a dull ache arising from unrequited love to those attendant upon violent mutilation that it has lost its significance. But the apostle of the word in its most physical connotation is Mr. Jeffers, who has so tortured his victims that we are glad they are only puppets being manipulated by the poet for his own satisfaction and are incapable of feeling the pain he enjoys inflicting. In general, the willing acceptance of pain comes from the added depth it gives to the qualities of love and mercy.

The search for security in a world of rapidly changing values is evident in the work of all except those poets who attained a full emotional and intellectual maturity normally, gradually, and painlessly. Undue emphasis has been given the anguish attendant upon the process of growing up and on the keen sufferings of youth. Too many young poets remain second- and third-rate because of their inability to suffer the pain poets of another generation seem to have suffered. This pseudo-suffering is sentimentalism of the worst type. The dissatisfaction with the present and a longing for the golden era is not so much nostalgia as it is the absence of historical perspective, particularly the perspective of social history.

To anyone who has been a serious reader of modern American poetry, one fact becomes increasingly clear. Ours is not a great age of poetry. We have many competent poets but few great ones. The general level of poetry is high, and the number of minor poems worthy survival is probably greater now than at any preceding age in America. We have only one poet who, I think, has great enough stature to become a major figure: Mr. Frost. In him alone I find the depth of thought, range of intellect, density of feeling, and artistic craftsmanship ably fused. His finished work is ample. Hart Crane has had perhaps the greatest poetic sensibility of any American poet. He had a quality of feeling, a genius for expression, and the capacity for self-criticism as an artist that, could his intellect and life have been disciplined, might have raised him to a great eminence. Mr. Wallace Stevens possesses the qualities of the artist and a highly developed and courageous intellect. What his poetry lacks—and this, of course, is only my own opinion—is the density that can only come from the controlled expression of an uninhibited emotion. I do not mean to suggest that his poetry lacks emotion; but I do think him to be too consciously reserved, too much the gentleman. He is afraid to let go.

It is by these three men, then—Mr. Frost, Mr. Stevens, and Hart Crane—that I believe our poetic height must be determined. The other poets in the present volume, and many not here included, form a plateau, although an uneven one. The poetic ground around the plateau is rough. Sometimes there are great gullies into which the newspaper-readers swarm for their poetic nourishment. Fortunately, the soil of these gullies is not harmful, and it often provides bits of homely wisdom and inspiration that are received with pleasure and profit. American poetry is coming of age, but the youthful quality that is everywhere evident in American life is still more evident than is desirable in some of our more important figures. Like our intellectual undergraduates, to quote Mr. Frost,

They will tell you more as soon as
You tell them what to do
With their ever breaking newness
And their courage to be new.

EMILY DICKINSON

(1830—1886)

EMILY DICKINSON is America's foremost woman poet; there is no second. Called by many one of the four greatest women poets of all time, few would dispute her claim. She has been grouped with Elizabeth Barrett Browning, with Christina Rossetti, and with Emily Brontë, a just estimate. She has been placed on the same peak with Sappho, but this is unfortunate. Any similarities are of the surface. Basically they have differences so great as to form an unbridgeable gulf between them. Both, it is true, have the same intensity of personal emotion. But in the fragments we have from Sappho the reader feels depth as well as height. With Emily Dickinson there is only height. What I have long sensed in her work is analogous to that felt by Mr. De Voto when he said of her poems that 'they are light without heat, they are flame without fire, they are splendour without substance—light as phosphorus, light as refracted by a diamond.' Mr. De Voto's statement that she is 'the supreme poet of hate' and that 'it is only by sifting and assaying complex hatreds that criticism will ever see her plain,' is meaningless to me.

The reader who has read all her published work will have a different attitude toward her from one who has only read her work in selection. She is a poet to be dipped into, not read for too long a time at one sitting. She knew what the reader soon becomes aware of, that more than any other poet, she repeats herself. 'While my thought is undressed,' she wrote to Higginson in 1862, 'I can make a distinction; but when I put them in a gown they look alike and numb.' Or, as she aptly expressed it in another connection, 'it is of realms unratified that magic is made.'

In selection, the sentimentalism of a large portion of her

work disappears and the reader loses sight of what becomes too apparent when her poetry is studied *en masse*.

Too many of her verses are the intense but vapid effusions of a person whose roots are not deep in life, of a sexually frustrated woman who concealed her frustration in a precious attitude of what she called sanity 'in a world *in*sane,' of one who shunned the earthly responsibilities of her own household 'except that bright one of faith,' of one who did not wish to grow up. Some readers think that by shunning the realities of everyday life, she found the greater reality in the realm of the spirit and imagination; that she found the 'ecstasy in living' greater when alone than was possible in the restricted society of the Amherst of her day, that she found life itself 'so startling' that she almost resented the necessity of personal contacts. She undoubtedly found greater happiness in her seclusion, in spite of her 'loneliness, perhaps too daily to relate,' than she would have experienced among the Amherst matrons with their small-talk of husbands, babies, cooking, and the minutiae of life. Had this seclusion come after her emotional nature had been fully developed she could have gained much. Coming before, however, her loss overshadows her gain. She missed the complete maturity that such contacts could have given her.

Although fully aware of the joy that could come from seclusion, I think she minimized the richness that could imperceptibly accrue to the person who through anonymous contacts with all strata of society gains a better perception of his own stratum, and, particularly, of himself in relation to it. She was justified in her opinion that to be able to be happy with one's own rich resources

> In an unfurnished circumstance,
> Possession is to one
> As an estate perpetual
> Or a reduceless mine.

But such a life is not enough. Her imaginative experiences gained in intensity by her seclusion, but the roots of these experiences failed to go deep into daily communal experience. Read continuously, her poetry causes the over-fatigue arising from too-long association with one who has not learned to let go. The sentimentalism, from a man's point of view at least, most clearly reveals itself in the display of an emotion greater than the occasion warrants. Her throat 'scalds' and 'blisters' too many times a day because of her love for her friends, for a flower, for a bee, or a bird. What is there left for the important crises? Any person living so constantly in this intense and rarefied air would burn herself out, would suffer nervous prostration as she did in 1884. But given a genuine crisis like death, womanlike, she faced the realities with a stoicism that confuses a man who has only seen women greatly upset over trivialities. At best this intensity was capable of but short flight. This, and not her absorption with her domestic duties, kept her from a sustained song longer than that of a few brief stanzas. If she is often precious it is because her food is too esoteric. She did not err in thinking the 'soul's superior instants' must be experienced alone. They must be. As she said, and truly said, 'exhilaration is within.' It is the foundation on which these instants rest that seems too fragile.

Innumerable poems reveal her inability to grasp the joy of reality. Such a poet may exercise a charm, but it will not last. 'That is best which is not,' she maintains in poem after poem; 'Achieve it' and 'you efface the sheen.' Because she denied herself the measure of relativity, she could not see how far she had yet to travel. The pitch of her flight is never that of an eagle, only occasionally that of a tercelet. At another time she has said that 'not to discover weakness is The mystery of strength.' More realistic would have been the strength that recognizes weakness, but sees the weakness in its true relationship to the other qualities.

She accustomed herself too completely to a life of memory. 'You cannot make remembrance grow When it has lost its root,' she wrote in a compelling lyric. She failed to see that the remembrances she attempted to make grow were themselves rootless. These several characteristics are all manifestations of the one basic fact that emotionally, Emily Dickinson never outgrew adolescence. I think Mrs. Bingham is correct in suggesting that 'from the very incompleteness of her experience may have sprung her love poems.' And that the statement is correct is a further attestation of adolescence. Mr. Whicher has taken the unnecessary pains to attempt to identify the men who may have been her inspiration. The more reserved or less intimate her contacts and the less specific basis on which to build castles, the larger and more luminous are apt to be her air castles. I think the men who inspired Emily's love poems are those she knew least. They, I am quite certain, never suspected that they were inspiring poems that would later cause so much speculation. She preferred the sorcery of surmising to the stark reality of seeing.

Mr. Whicher lists as one of 'the psychic pressures' that drove her to find relief in expression 'a sense of deprivation and loss as none of her attachments to young men matured into love and marriage, a catastrophic collapse of a dream of intellectual companionship that she too rashly allowed herself to entertain.' I think Mr. De Voto much closer to the truth by rejecting 'the shallow notion that Emily Dickinson's poems about love were love poems: that they came from any woman's desire for any man, least of all Emily's desire for George Gould or Charles Wadsworth. They and love—love as a longing of men and women, love as a wish for fulfilment, love as something possible to mortals, love as a richness or completion of the body, love that implies happiness or marriage or children—they and love are altogether incommensurable.'

Her love poems are her weakest because, in spite of the ecstatic and intense efforts made possible by the fusion of her imagination and intellect, they lack the solid basis of a rich and fruitful contact with the soil, and the acceptance of the homely interruptions and occurrences of daily life. This lack was no hindrance to her in her poems on death, immortality, and God. Love, for example, was not for her an acceptance of the daily responsibilities of house-keeping, child-bearing, and self-abnegation. She had, perhaps, too much of the first and last in her father's house. Love was an escape into realms of pure gold—an impossible ideal, of course, except to the adolescent. She demanded for herself a too rarefied air, and her poetry suffers for it. She found excuses for herself, I think, in an over-developed sense of duty to her father and mother. 'When father lived,' she wrote after his death, 'I remained with him because he would miss me. Now, mother is helpless, a holier demand.' She shunned life because she was afraid and rationalized the ever-tightening circumference of her material existence by the boldness with which she attacked some of the greater because unsolvable problems of the intellect. To be adolescent emotionally implies a distorted view of life—but this does not mean that the person is emotionally adolescent on all subjects, nor does it imply that she must remain intellectually adolescent. Emily Dickinson grew mentally to the very end. Remarks such as 'while Shakespeare remains, literature is firm,' 'biography first convinces us of the fleeing of the biographied,' and 'the only balmless wound is the departed human life we had learned to need'—indicate the direction and reaches of her thought.

These greater issues she could not shun, and her inability to do so gives the authentic ring of sincerity to her emotional and intellectual approach to the problems of death, immortality, and God. She resolutely faced the facts attendant upon the deaths of those close to her. Her basic integrity and inquiring mind made it impossible to avoid the questions that, unasked, might have left her childhood beliefs undisturbed. Painful though many of the implications were with which she wrestled, she faced them to the best of her ability. She transmuted the torture and anguish into lyrics of poignant and searching beauty. In these poems only does one occasionally sense the depth that in Mr. Frost's best poems is never absent. She could not learn acceptance.

To say this is not to say that she achieved an unwavering philosophy that enabled her to meet all crises. She did not. Like Hardy's musings on the imponderables, hers are often impressions rather than convictions. In times of stress she was forced back to her childhood faith; in times of peace she could journey with the most adventurous and intrepid traveller. She knew that captivity, like liberty, was consciousness, and that mind could make of life what it wished.

Travel though she might to the far reaches of the imagination, she preferred the factual life of her daily existence. The house of supposition, with the 'glimmering frontier that skirts the acre of perhaps,' revealed itself to her, she said, to be insecure. Many of her poems on the imponderables often have, however, as sentimental a cast as those on other subjects. They have this quality because of a loss of perspective. She too much resembles Miss Havisham in *Great Expectations* who shut herself from the actual world of men and women and lived alone with her memories. Were this not so, she could never have written that 'an actual suffering strengthens, As sinews do, with age,' and that

> Time is a test of trouble,
> But not a remedy.
> If such it prove, it prove too
> There was no malady.

Emily escaped behind physical barriers. To-day her spiritual sisters escape behind mental barriers that they take with them wherever they may go.

What characteristics do the poems possess, however, that give the vitality necessary for survival? Mrs. Bingham makes a desirable division of subject-matter under twelve main headings. These could be grouped under larger general headings. The first four primarily concern themselves with nature—with its grander aspects—dawn, sunrise, noon, massing clouds, slow-moving night, and so forth; with the mutation of the seasons; with the minutiae of nature—her garden's pageantry from spring to frost; and with animal life—frogs, birds, spiders, squirrels, rats, angleworms, insects, and snakes. The second four deal with people: children, mostly small boys; her own childhood and young-womanly experiences; specific persons she has known; her love poems. Except for those about nature in her grander aspects—and even some of these—the majority of the rest have what I feel to be a strongly sentimental cast. Many are clever and epigrammatic; they often seem to say more than they actually do. A careful rereading reveals their essential triviality. To a masculine reader, at least, they are those which could be most readily dispensed with. The last four contain her poems on death and her treatment of the larger generalizations. Here are her finest lyrics.

The reader can more easily apprehend some of the fundamental weaknesses of her poems in her letters; the basic qualities are the same. Her aphoristic style sparkles and glitters. Unfortunately, however, much of the glitter is that of paste rather than of a true jewel. A reader marks many, but soon deletes his marks because they do not survive several readings. Even most of the passages one troubles to transcribe quickly dull or tarnish. The surface brilliance is all. A reader soon detects a magnified self-consciousness—the same self-consciousness of one who too desperately tries to assert what he knows to be untrue. The false glitter of her letters, like that of the poems, is largely a problem of diction. As a poet she knew that she must seek the right word; and her manuscripts abundantly testify that she was diligent in her search. Her lexicon was for many years, she said, her 'only companion.' But however painstakingly she searched for the right word (and she 'probed philology') she was not invariably successful. She fails in the idiomatic use of words, and they assume under her hand an esoteric meaning which frequently renders a passage incomprehensible. Her choice at first startles and seems to carry profundity. Re-examination puzzles and confounds. What could she have meant? Instead of profundity, careful study reveals that many are little more than nonsense. They seem to have a crystalline clarity, but they are cloudy and confused.

This is often apparent in a poem which made a first sharp impact on the reader. I find elusive, for example, the second stanza of 'To undertake is to achieve.' Repeatedly I have experienced these undecipherable passages, and have not been alone in my reactions. The first stanza is often clear, brilliant, and penetrating. But unless I am constantly alert, I am apt to let the clarity of one stanza blind me to the confused statement of the second. Every word seems simple, the syntax is orderly and direct, and it sounds clear. The meaning, however, is not. Several contemporary poets are guilty of this same obscurity. It occurred frequently in Auden's earlier work and is occasional in his later. Lesser young poets have attempted to make it a virtue. Emily Dickinson has the same difficulty in crystallizing an originally clear idea as she has in avoiding repetition. What, for example, is the meaning lying behind the flashy façade of 'nature is a haunted house, but art a house that tries to be haunted'? Is she speaking of the mystery of nature?

Recognizing these weaknesses for what they are—and, strangely enough, they are often her strength—how did they affect her work? The most obvious influence is in her prosodic structure. Her most dominant verse is the tetrameter, with the trimeter second in importance. Her stanzas, however, are a multiplicity of types, all rather short. The quatrain is her favourite. The reader experiences a sense of relief when on a rare occasion she lengthens her tetrameter line as in 'He preached upon breadth.' Her vowels are overwhelmingly high and front—vowels of intensity rather than of relaxation; her consonants are strongly infused with liquids, nasals, and sibilants. These sounds in the smaller forms bolster the intensity of her emotion. After much reading of her poetry one hungers for the pentameter or longer lines, for heavier vowels, and retarding consonants. One yearns for the more comfortable, earthy talk of men pitched an octave lower, and wants less of the fervour of a person too conscious and too worried by the frugality of time to live, of one who finds that her own words so 'chill and burn' her that 'the temperature of other minds is too new an awe,' whatever that may mean.

The simple directness of her statement—so different from most of the contemporary poetry of her day—is forceful in its terseness. That it is natural to her is evident from her letters with their flashing pages so often lacking in perspective. 'Friday I tasted life,' she wrote; cleverly, no doubt, but too obviously and studiously clever. 'It was a vast morsel. A circus passed the house—still I feel the red in my mind though the drums are out'; and she gave further expression to the experience in a poem. Many times, in fact, the prose of her letters falls into the pattern of her verse, or could be made to do so with only a slight alteration. Her style gives us as vivid a picture of her as we need. It has fervour and simplicity with little of the worldling about it, but much of the *poseuse*. I think that, partly as a result of the early praise of her school friends who recognized and encouraged her literary ability, she developed the self-consciousness that pervades so much of her work. In the early years she strove for 'fancy,' as when she wrote, 'My heart grows light so fast that I could mount a grasshopper and gallop around the world, and not fatigue him any.' Fancy later gave way to imagination. And although she rarely showed her verses and never published a selection of her poems, she was not unconscious or undesirous of fame. Only the inexperienced saves all his scraps. At her best she rises above her self-consciousness and grants us glimpses of a soul of complete integrity and naturalness. Her soul attempted so long, however, to make a virtue of fear that she forgot that she was a caged skylark and mistook the dull bars of her cage for heaven's gates. In the ecstasy of her vision her voice swelled into a vibrant lyricism, which, enhanced by her analogizing powers, gives her her greatest claim to fame.

Her imagery has received frequent attention. It has been called bold and startling. More merited praise would have recognized its integrity. It springs from her own narrowly restricted physical activities. She was artist enough to recognize that she could analogize only those things she knew intimately if she were to avoid a sense of pastiche, patchwork, or insincerity. The so-called boldness of her imagery is only a manifestation of her circumscribed life. She could illumine and explain cosmic matters only by their reduction to the little daily tasks that engrossed her or to the life of Amherst being lived about her. No poet was so aware of the minutiae of her daily life as was she, and perhaps no one so unconscious that they were minutiae and not milestones. Whether the moon sustained in 'independent amber' 'rides like a girl through a topaz town,' or butterflies 'off banks of noon' 'leap plashless as they swim,' or the seraphs 'swing their snowy hats,' we can be certain that she speaks from her own experience. The Amherst landlord turning out the town drunk stirred her memory in later years to speak of the 'drunken bee' being turned 'out of the foxglove's door.'

Domestic moments are a rich mine for her images. Cookery furnishes many: 'surprise,' for example, 'is like a thrilling pungent Upon a tasteless meat,' and 'impossibility' is like

c

wine in its powers of exhilaration, but 'possibility' is 'flavour-less'; the soul is compared to 'ripening fruit' or to a 'banquet.' Typical is the following passage from a poem on a single sustained image from sewing:

> To mend each tattered faith
> There is a needle fair:
> Though no appearance indicate
> 'Tis threaded in the air.

A soul, too, has 'bandaged' moments: shame is a 'shawl of pink.' She speaks of brushing off the summer 'as housewives do a fly' or of 'sweeping up the heart' after the death of a dear one.

As we should expect from one whose garden circumscribed her physical world, images from flowers and garden inhabitants are abundant. Remembrance will not grow, for example, 'when it has lost its root'; and arid pleasure differs from joy 'as frost is different from dew'; and a narrow escape tingles in the mind 'like paragraphs of wind.' No reader can be unaware of the significance to her of this cultivated area. Many of the more than forty-one species of flowers chosen equally from the cultivated and wild have provided images. Her favourite inhabitants are the small creatures, including the butterfly, crickets, house-flies, bees, and others. Mr. Whicher has pointed out the extensive range of her sensory and imaginative use of the bee—colour, motion, sound, touch, taste, kinaes-thesis;[1] gaiety, fancy, humour, hyperbole, sentiment, symbol, mystery, solemnity, and benediction. Grief, for example, is a mouse; the heaven we chase is likened to a bee pursued by a schoolboy; and how dreary, she says, to be public 'like a frog.' She described the sound of the bee, too, as 'like trains of cars on tracks of plush,' and compares a beetle on the ceiling to a bomb.

Childhood fascinated her and afforded numerous analogies to

[1] Kinaesthesis: the sense of muscular effort.

life. Bliss is a thing of a child. The soul in pain 'puts his play-
things up,' earth is but a 'scanty toy,' and faith is likened to
one who 'slips and laughs and rallies.'

Ritual, too, attracted her. Indian summer is a sacrament;
'one mitred afternoon' awaits everyone, and wings of butterfly are like an 'assumption gown.' Several images are from her
reading, and the results sometimes border on the bizarre.
Such is the effect when she uses 'chivalries' instead of 'cour-
tesies' or 'gifts': 'By chivalries as tiny As blossoms or a book.'
Or when she speaks of 'massacres' as 'soft' in a couplet that
illustrates her use of sibilants in alliteration: 'Soft as the
massacre of suns By evening's sabres slain.' Even a glance at
the first lines of the poems will furnish many others. Certainly
she was as conscious an imagist as any of that coterie that so
labelled themselves.

A further glance at her first lines would likewise disclose
the important rôle played by personification in her work.
It is neither stilted, nor dead, nor of literary origin. It is fresh
and compelling, although it may appeal more to the childlike
quality in man than to his mature nature. Oxymorons, too,
are frequent and lend much of the startling quality to her
verse, as in 'How ruthless are the gentle! How cruel are the
kind!'

Whatever passion for truth Emily Dickinson may have had
manifests itself in her definitions that constitute so large a
part of her poetry, although the smack of self-consciousness
is greater here than anywhere else. Those of 'fame,' for
example, of 'paradise,' 'patience,' or of 'love.' Fame is 'a
fickle food,' is 'the one that does not stay,' is 'the tint the
scholars leave.' Paradise is 'that old mansion'; patience 'has a
quiet outer'; love 'is that later thing than death.' Every reader
will make mental notes of others that appeal to him. Definitions frequently occur, too, in her letters, and often with a
simplicity more forceful than in a poem. She was not blinded
by familiar words. She analysed them. Witness her definition

of 'mother': 'I suppose a mother is one to whom you hurry when you are troubled.' 'Home,' she wrote, 'is so far from home, since my father died.'

In an age when assonance and half-rhymes were carefully avoided, she employed them knowing their value for certain emotional effects. Her first editor, Mrs. Todd, often silently 'improved' a stanza by altering the original manuscript to achieve a perfect rhyme when none was intended. Her most recent editor, Mrs. Bingham, scholarly in her treatment of the originals, has made it possible for us to see more clearly than before Miss Dickinson's intense sensitivity to subtle verbal harmonies.

The influences on her work and thought were many. Emerson and Thoreau were familiar to her. She felt the deep spell of George Eliot and the Brontës. Shakespeare provided her with a world more real than that which passed her gate. Like Blake, however, the form of her poetry seems to have its source from within herself. Certainly there is little of Keats, of the Brownings, of Ruskin, Thomas Browne, and *Revelations* that she told Higginson were her books. Perhaps in no poet is there less consciousness of the verbal influence of others. She never consciously, she said, touched 'a paint mixed by another person.' This is merely another way of calling attention to herself. The condensation of her experience dictated the form, and she could not help it if the failure of a rhyme disappointed her reader.

Nevertheless, though a reader may object to many of her limitations, and to the particular esoteric uses to which she sometimes puts her words, he must recognize that she has a feeling for words in relation to one another that might well be the envy of other poets whose roots went deeper. Although in a different key from Wordsworth (at his rare best), she possesses his sense of the inevitability of words in conjunction.

From the point of view of her artistic achievement her greatest lack is magnitude. The aesthetic impact of her best work is that made by a beautiful miniature. At its best, it is above criticism. Too much of it, however, is the crystallization of isolated moments, rather than the ever ripening expression of a person who through steady contact with life gradually realizes, as has Mr. Frost, that though the scientific facts reported in *Genesis* might grow obsolete, the fundamental truths remain. Perhaps it was not her fault, but a fault of the times, of the nature of Amherst in general, and of her own home environment in particular. Whatever the reasons, Emily Dickinson can never take her place as a great major poet, but she will remain among the best of the minor ones. The narrowness of her world was chiefly narrowness in the physical sense. Intellectually she was fearless and daring. Her poems on death and immortality are ample proof of that. But the unconscious restrictions which she placed on the reach of her intellectual powers could not be overcome. She failed to grasp the significance of the myth of Antaeus who was invincible as long as he was in contact with his mother Earth. No poet can neglect this myth. The absence of this continuous touch keeps her from imparting to one reader, at least, the sense of depth. She is as truly New England as is Mr. Frost; but it is a phase of New England that only one with New England roots can fully understand, a casual visitor never. It is a phase that, though it moves in the open, lives as truly in the circumscribed limits of the Dickinson house and garden as did Emily.

Emily Dickinson's influence has been great on contemporary poets, particularly on the small group of capable women poets who have frequently caught the intensity that pervades her work. Because she was free from the florid extravagance that was the bane of the painting, music, architecture, and poetry of her day, the moderns in their search for functionalism have enlisted her support. She has played a unique rôle in restoring to poetry those important characteristics of simplicity, sensuousness, and passion.

EDWIN ARLINGTON ROBINSON

(1869—1935)

A POET'S admirers generally quarrel with an antholo-gist's selection of his work. Their particular favourites, they feel, are invariably omitted. With the selections from Edwin Arlington Robinson, however, there can be little disagreement. Although he was one of the most prolific poets of his age—there are almost 1,500 pages in his *Collected Poems*—the number of poems meriting survival is relatively small, and none of them is long—not longer than 'Ben Jonson Entertains a Man from Stratford,' 'Isaac and Archibald,' or 'The Man Against the Sky.' His failure will not be because of his shortcomings as a thinker—although I think he has been overrated as a psychologist—but because of his failure as an artist. Too many persons confuse over-attentuation with profundity.

From the point of view of poetic method, Robinson is at the end of a tradition—that of Tennyson, Browning, and the pre-Raphaelites. Like Hardy he was searching for natural speech-rhythms. From the point of view of subject-matter, Robinson sought to do for the American scene what Hardy was successfully doing for the English—he attempted to make the common experiences of American life a fit subject for poetry. This, of course, is also in the tradition of Whitman. Like Hardy, however, he was following the general tradition of the nineteenth-century novelists instead of the poets. More particularly, he was carrying on the extremely subtle psychologizing of George Meredith and Henry James and the realism of William Dean Howells. His historical impor-tance to American poetry is significant, whatever may be his final stature as a poet.

Among the common experiences in which he was

interested, failure most persistently furnished him his subject-matter. The failures he particularly enjoyed writing about were those which result from excessive idealism rather than from too little. They have seen the gleam, but through some paralysis of will, inability to face crass materialism, blemish of intelligence, or trick of fate, were unable to transfer their idealism to action until it either was—or almost was—too late. Many had no desire to change and achieved a final reconciliation. The failure may have been that of Leffing-well—

> What quiverings in the distance of what light
> May not have lured him with high promises
> And then gone down?
>
> 'Leffingwell' (I. The Lure)

Or it may have been the failure of Clavering who 'clung to phantoms and to friends, And never came to anything,' or that of Miniver Cheevy, Mr. Flood, or that of any one of a score of others. It is a mood of 'optimistic desperation.' Although unable to recognize the truth in time to save themselves, their example could divert others from a similar fate. The Flammondes, Captain Craigs, Miniver Cheevys, Richard Corys, and Roman Bartholows that throng his pages under different guises, different names, and different backgrounds, may or may not have failed from the world's materialistic point of view—that of outward prosperity and happiness—but each has failed. Often it is because of their inability to get an objective view of themselves—in other words, because they lacked a sense of humour. Their failure was Robinson's own failure. In spite of a keenly ironic humour toward the incidents that lay outside of themselves, they had little humour about themselves. The failures may have been acquaintances that Robinson observed; as often they are persons he had read about. Except in his shorter poems, almost no case that I can recall, in spite of psychological probing and dialectic on the poet's part, is about a person into whose soul he has entered. He has the great defect, in his long poems particularly, of a lack of empathy.[1] He never merges his personality in that of one of the characters. He never wholly understands him however minutely he may have observed him.

His preoccupation with psychologic nuance is not only a basic weakness, it is often his undoing. It is apparent in 'Captain Craig,' becomes more pronounced in 'The Book of Anandale,' and achieves insufferable proportions in 'Roman Bartholow' and several of his later longer poems. The absence of significant form from these longer poems becomes more pronounced with the years, and the reader soon realizes that no poet so cries out for condensation. Instead of repeated rereadings of Robinson bringing out hidden and subtle beauties, as is the case with Mr. Frost, his automatic technique for producing his effects is soon so apparent that the reader experiences the poet's own fatigue with his mechanical labours. He is stifled by the poet's basic lack of sincerity as an artist. It was a barren age of poetry, or an extremely uncritical audience, that could give them stature and spread over them an aura that continues to persist.

It is, moreover, obvious from his own account that he was too facile a writer. We read in his letters of 250 lines being written in three days, 500 in eight days ('Lancelot'), of 1,000 in two weeks ('Merlin'), and so on. As a first draft to be subjected to careful revision this might be understandable; but only might. When we read further, however, and discover that to 3,000 lines, written in a comparatively short period, he gave only a month to revision, the reason for the lack of density of his lines is clear. He was content that after such reworking, the work would 'be as good and as bad as he was likely to make it.' The artist's capacity for self-criticism as regards form was not highly developed.

The weaknesses are, of course, both more apparent and

[1] Empathy: the imaginative identification of oneself with another person or group.

more abundant in the long poems. Let us, then, first examine these, reserving for final discussion those against which time has not so far made too deep inroads. These long poems are written in a blank verse that changed only slightly with the years. No inner necessity impelled Robinson to new forms. The early poems in this meter have the unmistakable ring of the dramatic monologues of Browning, but an attenuated Browning become slightly tinkling. Robinson is not so robust. He denied Browning's influence on his work although admitting that of Wordsworth and Kipling. The influence may not have been conscious on his part, but it is none the less present—subconsciously perhaps. Passages from his letters of 1894 and 1898 reveal that he read him extensively.

His vocabulary is strongly polysyllabic, too much so. An occasional passage like the following from 'Captain Craig' would pass unnoticed:

> But at length
> He found himself and soon began to chant,
> With a fitful shift at thin sonorousness
> The jocund instrument; and had he been
> Definitively parceling to us
> All Kimberley and half of Ballarat,
> The lordly quaver of his poor old words
> Could not have been more magniloquent.
>
> p. 149

This, of course, is not poetry. It is prose, broken up into lines of ten syllables, and bad prose at that. But when polysyllabic passages like this occur monotonously through hundreds of pages after hundreds of pages the reader, long before he has reached the end, wishes that Robinson had curbed his prolixity, had hammered out some lines with density or tightness of texture. A small fraction of his output more carefully wrought would have assured him greater longevity.

The foregoing passage illustrates another characteristic,

too, that Robinson overdoes: his tendency to run-on lines. At times, even in one of his better poems like 'Ben Jonson, etc.,' three or four lines gallop or plod on (as the case may be) with no end caesura and often with no medial one. Again were this a rare occurrence it could be used with striking effect, but in his longer poems it occurs so repeatedly that any possible strong impact is lost.

A third weakness of Robinson, more evident in his blank verse than elsewhere, is his use of repetition, generally in what might be called a 'turn.'[1] This becomes such a set stylistic device that before the reader is fully conscious of the fact he is almost counting the number of 'turns' to the page. When I first read 'Tristram' more than twenty years ago I was conscious of this device. When rereading Robinson for the purposes of the present essay I realized that compared with the other long poems 'Tristram' was relatively free from them. There, at least, they did not put a barrier between the reader and his subject-matter. Opening *Collected Poems* at random, we are confronted with the following passage in 'Merlin':

> For now to Merlin, in his paradise,
> Had come an unseen angel with a sword
> Unseen, the touch of which was a long fear
> For longer sorrow that had never come,
> Yet might if he compelled it. He discovered
> One golden day in autumn as he wandered,

[1] By a 'turn' I mean the poet's skill in playing with a recurrent word, phrase and cadence. Generally the element at the end of one line recurs at the beginning of the following. The following passage from Spenser's *Faerie Queene* illustrates his manner of weaving intricate patterns by the use of 'turns':

> Amongst those knights there were three brethren bold,
> Three bolder brethren never were yborne,
> Borne of one mother in one happie mold,
> Borne at one burden in one happie morne,
> Thrise happie mother, and thrise happie morne,
> That bore three such, three such not to be fond. (IV, ii, 41.)

That he had made the radiance of two years
A misty twilight when he might as well
Have had no mist between him and the sun,
The sun being Vivian.

p. 286

The repetition of 'come,' 'unseen,' 'long'—'longer,' 'misty'—
'mist,' and 'sun' throws a dreamlike quality over the whole.
It may even induce in the inattentive reader the sense that
Robinson is being profound when he is only being prolix
in his suggestiveness and suffering auto-intoxication from
the sound of his own voice. The picture of Merlin and
Vivian are impressionistic—like those of the other Arthurian
characters in 'Lancelot' and 'Tristram'—almost Debussy-like;
but they lack Debussy's sensitive control of his medium and,
even more, his vitality. Perhaps an even better example of
Robinson's pseudo-profundity is the passage beginning 'He
paused and would have hesitated longer' ('Merlin,' p. 288,
5 lines).

What is true of 'Merlin' is even truer of 'Lancelot.' The
characters have no dimension and are dream-figures. This
dreamlike quality is enhanced by his manner of telling the
story which without some familiarity with Malory would be
difficult to follow. The outline is not clear. More serious,
however, is the fact that there is not a single tightly wrought
passage in the entire poem.

Between 'Lancelot' (1920) and 'Tristram' (1927) Robinson
reached the height of his mannered and monotonous verse
in 'Roman Bartholow' in which the language of each of the
characters is pitched in the same key. Each is so prolix that
I am certain no character would have had the patience to
listen to the other. The whole lacks vitality and variation.
Here, crowding every page, are examples of a style that
had become a habit and from which every vestige of inspira-

tion has vanished. They possess a deadly flatness. Two examples will suffice, one short, the other more extended:

> things of common use,
> That lay as they had lain there before clouds
> Had wrapt her days with night and stifled them
> Till day was night within her and around her.
>
> p. 786

> Gabrielle heard the moths outside the screen,
> Still angry at their freedom, while she faced
> A freedom hardly worth another anger
> That she felt rising in her at herself,
> For being herself.
>
> p. 795

In 'Tristram,' where Robinson took the same licence with his source-material as in his other Arthurian poems, his polysyllabism does not beat so insistently as it has heretofore done and his use of repetition is not so laboured as it has been, even though he still overdoes it. He has become too facile in certain techniques reaching him from Spenser via Tennyson, and he has not suffused his words with the strong passion that makes them come alive. The spirit is wanting. Unfortunately, such passages abound as 'The fires of love and fear Had slowly burned away so much of her' (p. 672), and more particularly the following:

> They were not made for time as others were,
> And time therefore would not be long for them
> Wherein for love to learn that in their love,
> Where fate was more than time and more than love,
> Time never was, save in their fear of it—
> Fearing, as one, to find themselves again
> Intolerably as two that were not there.
>
> p. 675

When the reader is confronted with some of the long-winded conversations between Tristram and Isolt before the consummation of their love one questions whether or not Robinson actually understood love, whether he was the psychologist some have thought him to be. Such conversations as theirs would have killed passion, not augmented it. Some modification of the conversation reported in Section VII might possibly have taken place *after* the consummation; certainly *not before*.

There is less of the dead level of prosiness in 'Tristram' than elsewhere in the long poems, and the beginning of Section VIII is much better than other parts. In fact, I think the sensitive reader must perforce recognize that Robinson's blank verse is, as I have already suggested, essentially rhythmical prose. Even the 'rhythmical' is sometimes lacking; certainly any inner tension is wanting. What is true of the long poems before and including 'Tristram' is even more true of those following—'Cavender's House,' 'The Glory of the Nightingales,' and others. When he forced himself to write these he was in a state of poetic exhaustion.

It is true that Robinson has put a distinctive stamp on his blank verse, but it is a stamp that should have no imitators. It is romanticism grown threadbare. It is the music of Mahler without Mahler's variety or frequent moments of pure inspiration. The basic weaknesses arise from the poet's lack of domination and control of his materials. He has let himself spread out over the muddy flats rather than confine himself within definite limits. In spite of a superficial outline, the long poems suffer from a lack of significant form. They are literary exercises rather than passionate experiences. Frankly, I don't think they are worth reading. Obviously, I cannot agree with Mr. Cestre's glowing account of these long poems (1930). They have the same 'refrigerating effect' on me that Robinson wrote 'Merlin' had had on the critics. 'Lancelot' has been called 'a poignant regret at the inevitable passing of beauty; a pathetic acknowledgement of the failure of human relationships, a profound conviction of the ultimate efficacy of moral idealism.' 'Merlin' represents, it is said, 'the breakdown of intelligence as an instrument wherewith man might control experiences'; and both 'Lancelot' and 'Merlin' are 'necessarily pictures of a world in solution' (Morris, *The Poetry of Edwin Arlington Robinson*). But a reader of to-day is hard put to it to find the symbolism apparent to those who read the poems at the end of the first World War. Robinson recognized a weakness of poets and philosophers, but did not heed what he knew:

> 'Whenever your poet or your philosopher
> Has nothing richer for us,' he resumed,
> 'He burrows among remnants, like a mouse
> In a waste-basket, and with much dry noise
> Comes up again, having found Time at the bottom
> And filled himself with its futility.
>   'Avon's Harvest,' p. 559

The reader, too, is filled with this sense of futility. Boccaccio may have been correct in calling poetry Philosophy's maid-servant, but in Robinson's house, the maidservant is too often a slattern.

If the long poems merit oblivion—and it was these that made of him a best-seller—what of the shorter poems? Here the critic can be less severe. At least two of the semi-long poems merit attention: 'Ben Jonson Entertains a Man from Stratford' and 'Isaac and Archibald.' The first is a sensitive appreciation of Shakespeare, and the other an effective idyll revealing Robinson's understanding of youth and old age. Poetically, 'Isaac and Archibald' is superior because the poet more completely merges himself in his subject. In spite of the polysyllabism of 'Ben Jonson,' however, Robinson's literary taste makes it a pleasant poem for the person who understands his Shakespeare. It demands more from the reader than almost any other of his poems; and anyone unacquainted with Shakespeare is likely to find it incomprehensible. Its interest lies in an attitude toward Shakespeare that the reader takes to the poem. He will find no new illumination, but he will find the standard ideas on Shakespeare expressed with control, frequently with imagination. In this, more than in any other of Robinson's dramatic monologues, there is less echo of Browning. When he attempts a similar poem on a painter he is not so successful. His 'Rembrandt to Rembrandt' not only lacks the psychologic insight of Browning in his 'Andrea del Sarto,' but tends to diffuseness. Rembrandt did not mean to him what Shakespeare did.

Robinson's claim on posterity will lie chiefly with the shorter poems and sonnets found in the volumes *The Children of the Night* (1890–1897), *The Town Down the River* (1910), and *The Man Against the Sky* (1916), with a very few from *Captain Craig* (1902) and *Avon's Harvest* (1921). We must not expect from Robinson, however, any prosodic innovations, although he does occasionally succeed in impressing his own personality on traditional forms. In such poems as 'Flammonde,' 'Richard Cory,' 'Miniver Cheevy,' and other well-known ones, admittedly his best, he has invested the traditional forms with a unique vitality. In far too many, however, and this is particularly true of some of the sonnets, he has given nothing to them. 'A Song at Shannon's,' for example, expresses one of his favourite and arresting themes that each of us is essentially alone. This sonnet, however, has a flabbiness of texture that robs it of its effectiveness. More than any other modern poet, Robinson needed the restraining force of a definite stanza-pattern. It is not surprising that some of his most successful poems are his sonnets.

In his long poems his images are often inappropriate, or at

least too facile. Although the following appear in a dream where anything can happen, it is bad:

> Tears
> Rolled out at last like bullets from his eyes
> And I could hear them fall down on the floor
> Like shoes.

'Captain Craig,' p. 163

Even less effective is the statement that the old man's eyes 'glittered like those Of a glad fish' (p. 160). 'Glad' is unfortunate. He also makes a pretty bad pun when he said that Morgan, for example,

> Was in the mood for almost anything
> From Bach to Offenbach

p. 168

Such infelicities, fortunately, do not often appear in the shorter poems, which in this respect are frequently more successful than the longer ones. After a separation of many years two old friends try to renew their contact. The failure, for example, is aptly caught in the image 'They dredged an hour for words, and then were done.' 'Glittered' and 'imperially slim' are effective when applied to Richard Cory, although they lack the inevitability of epithets we find in poets of greater stature. They also smack of the lamp. The fourth 'thought' in 'Miniver Cheevy,' especially the placing of the final one at the beginning of a line, is a master stroke. Particularly effective, too, are certain sections of 'Mr. Flood's Party'—his careful setting down of the jug, and the toast—and the sonnet, 'The Sheaves,' both of which poems continue to unfold themselves with rereading.

In one respect, however, Robinson showed himself a poet. He knew that words wear with time and that their meanings become blurred. A poet, being a dealer in words, must keep his stock fresh and their meanings accurate. He must also know when to use the simple rather than a baroque one.

Robinson attempted to keep his communication accurate by searching for words with incisiveness. He enriched his vocabulary from many sources. Had he been as careful in selecting the words to surround his less usual ones he might have achieved more. As Horace has pointed out, giving freshness to a familiar word is often better than searching for the unusual one. His greatest defect must remain, I think, a defect in his capacity for giving expression to deep feeling. He wrote too much and did not give to his revisions what was necessary to transmute them into great poetry. Even in these shorter poems, in which the iambic beat is frequently too pronounced, successive readings uncover the fact that although competent in fitting his thought to traditional verses, he is too facile a craftsman. Elsewhere I have made a similar charge against Hardy, but in comparison Hardy was a giant. It would have been better had Robinson moulded the forms to fit his thought as a truly original poet inevitably is forced to do—as Mr. Frost, for example, has so unobtrusively done. In *The Three Taverns* (1920), a collection of shorter poems, the careful reader discovers oratory rather than poetry. Robinson is far more successful in his Italian sonnets than elsewhere. Although he has made no contribution to the form, the form itself has imposed upon him a discipline that brought out the best he had to offer. Any selection of his work in anthologies reveals a preponderance of sonnets. In this medium he was restricted in his ability to 'play around the circumstance a little' and he achieved a tightness of texture that is elsewhere lacking. Many of these are in fact epigrams and good ones. 'Credo' is more deeply passionate than most, and 'New England' one of his best.

I mentioned earlier that Robinson often sacrificed significant form—that careful integration of thought, word, image, and prosodic pattern—for psychologic subtlety. This calls for elaboration. Much of his psychologizing is, as I have hinted, attenuated James. I have suggested that his understanding

D

of a deeply passionate love is wanting. He is better in his understanding of women. Merlin's speech to Vivian beginning, 'Why do you seize the flimsiest of opportunities' ('Merlin,' pp. 292, 293, 17 lines), reveals a sure insight into Vivian's mind and character. Each reader will find other passages with which to agree. Robinson is too apt, however, to over-subtilize his characters. Does he, for example, really understand Paul ('On The Way') or John Brown ('John Brown')? Both poems are weak Browning. His unique contribution to American poetry must be found in his 'reports' of his failures.

After the earliest volumes, and even often in these, the reader becomes conscious of the fact that Robinson does not write because he must. He remains too cool, too aloof. He gives the impression of a conscious search for material to versify. Everywhere the literary background is strong. Few poets are so widely read in the classics, in the Bible (particularly the Old Testament), or in medieval romance as was he. At least, none makes so constant a reference to it. My first intention was to say that he has consciously paraded his knowledge, but I think that would be unfair. He had a retentive memory and the allusions came, I am sure, almost spontaneously at need. Where he differs from a man like Mr. Frost, however, is that in Mr. Frost these things have been made more completely a part of himself. Rarely do I feel that Robinson's subject-matter is inevitable. Were it so his verses would possess the inner tension they so sorely need.

One of the tests of a good poem is that however often it is read it continues to yield an ever-increasing pleasure and understanding. I have found this true with all the great poets that time has raised to their present pre-eminence. I have found it to be true with Mr. Frost, and to a great extent with Mr. Stevens. I have found it to be so with poets whose subject-matter may be uncongenial or repellent. I have not found it true of Robinson.

His present high reputation is essentially a carry-over from the early enthusiasm for 'Tristram.' In the light in which the tradition of poetry has been altered during the intervening twenty years the danger to any poet willing to work wholly within the tradition of his immediate forebears, rather than take the arduous road of altering that tradition, is apparent from a rereading of his poetry. A rereading of his poetry has brought out an even greater danger. It is one which we in America generally fail to see, much less to heed. One generation cannot accept the dicta of its immediate predecessors, or, for that matter, of any earlier generation, on the work of any writer, painter, musician, architect, or anyone in the fine arts. Each must examine for itself, and must find a fresh message in his work. We must look behind our father's saying. What may have been alive in his day may since have died.

ROBERT FROST
(1875—   )

I. POET OF LOVE

ONLY by the attempt to view a poet's work as a whole can his true measure be taken. Or, as Hardy said, not until the last line has been written. The qualities manifest in Mr. Frost's latest poem, *The Masque of Mercy*, are such that it is not likely that any further poems will appreciably alter the conclusions now possible about his work. Read chronologically, Mr. Frost's poetry, like that of every true genius, reveals the steady and almost imperceptible mutations demanded by inner necessity, not those arising from external causes. Mr. Frost has always been a truly intellectual poet: thoughtful, not bookish; independent, not a mere sounding board for others' thoughts. His intellectual qualities are as apparent in his images, rhythms, and forms as in the rational content. Few poets have ranged wider or deeper in their reading of the great works than he.

He has been called the poet of New England. In its larger sense this limits him as much as it would to call Dante the poet of Catholicism; Shakespeare the poet of Elizabethan England; Milton the poet of Puritan England. In a narrow sense it is true. He writes, as does every sincere artist, from the background that he knows and of the different types of persons he has found there. But he is never strictly regional. The facts he selects from the microcosm of New England and its people are fundamental and true of the macrocosm. When he writes of love, for example, it is the fulfilment, frustration, or loss of love conditioned by a New England background; but the emotions are universal.

It has not always been recognized that love is a dominant

note in his poetry. The purity of his love is everywhere evident. When he once wrote that poetry was once more itself and back in love, it was not of his own poetry that he was thinking, but of the changing vicissitudes that love has undergone in poetry in general. His own poetry had never left love.

Love with Mr. Frost, however, is no vague generalization that at best can stir the reader only to some form of autobiographic musing. Generalizations are, in fact, impossible. As he himself said, 'There is no love,' by which he meant no abstraction called love that one could talk about. Love is a concrete thing and has meaning only in concrete terms. According to his statement in 'Build Soil,'

> There's only love of men and women, love
> Of children, love of friends, of men, of God,
> Divine love, human love, parental love,
> Roughly discriminated for the rough.

The foregoing types of love can, of course, only be 'roughly discriminated for the rough.' And certainly to attempt an explanation of one category—the love between men and women—will permit of no finely drawn clean-cut division; yet every rereading of Mr. Frost brings into clearer focus his preoccupation with love as it occurs between men and women. More and more insistently it beats upon the reader's consciousness. Love inspired the first poem in *Collected Poems* and has continued to inspire a group of poems in every subsequent volume, although the treatment has never remained the same. Only in *North of Boston*, however, are the poems on love and the reverse side of love widely separated. This is not to say that, like Hardy, he has interested himself in the tragedies and ironies of love as well as in its happier moments, although he recognizes the effects on love of fear. Nor is he chiefly interested, as was Lawrence, in those moments of intense struggle between lovers anxious and yet reluctant to surrender themselves to love. Nor was he interested, as were both Lawrence and Hardy, in the moments at the end of love—those moments when love has ended for one and not for the other. Such episodes were contrary to his own experiences, and however much they may hold interest for him, he was, fortunately, only occasionally interested in them as subject-matter for his own poetry. To suggest, therefore, that his treatment never remains the same is to mean that from the horizontal point of view he has kept his range narrow. His vertical range goes deep and rises to great heights.

Of all the poets writing to-day Mr. Frost, alone, seems to me to have something new to say on a phase of love that rarely receives consideration. I know of only one other poet who has captured the fine sensuousness of love at its highest as he has done, and that person, strangely as it may appear to some, was Milton in the early Paradise scenes of *Paradise Lost*. Yet it is not strange, either. Milton was, and Mr. Frost is, a Puritan in the best sense of the word; as Spenser was, and even as Keats was. These men possess one quality in common —their sensuousness. And I say this in the knowledge that an earlier critic has said of Mr. Frost that no poet is so little sensuous as he.

Mr. Frost resembles Milton, too, in the purity and innocence that attend his sensuousness. The love poetry of both is fresh, clean, passionate, and highly evocative.

If we are to understand the love between men and women in Mr. Frost's poetry we must remember that it is a part of his creed that a poet should 'make a late start to market.' He should not try to cash in by selling the hay that should be ploughed under for fertilizer any more than that he should sell his topsoil. He has little sympathy with poets who under the guise of love bring to market their biological experiments in sensation; one might almost say their sensational experiments in biology. Mr. Frost probably wrote many youthful love poems, but since he did not publish his first volume until he was thirty-seven and a married man with children, his natural taste and reticence prevented his publishing these early effusions. His critical judgement recognized that important as they might be in his own development, the world would be none the poorer without them. At best they were probably either misunderstood, vicarious, or imperfectly crystallized experiences. His sanity never permitted him a still more flagrant error. He could not see that a man had to fill his soul with 'sick and miserable experiences, self-imposed and self-inflicted, and greatly enjoyed, before he can sit down and write a lyric of strange and compelling beauty.' His willingness to restrict his own experiences to clean and healthy ones makes him burrow deeper to their fuller meaning. He conserved his energies, to be expended at the right moment.

Because Mr. Frost does not invariably write in the first person we must not overlook the essentially subjective quality of many outwardly objective poems; nor must we overlook the metaphorical implications which become ever more pronounced as the poet ripens. Ripens? Mellows? Ages? None is the really adequate word to describe the subtle gradations in work that is everywhere mature. The changes are such as come to a man as the mass of experiences behind him realistically conditions him to experiences yet to come.

But, whether early or late, his love poems never impress the reader because of their cunning, but because of their faith. One rarely feels that they are the result of his watching other lovers, but are rather the carefully wrought expression of his own deeply felt passion. Whether the poet writes in the first person or the third, whether he uses the given name of Warren, the surname Stark, or implies that it is Robert Frost, the results are the same and something unique in literature. The hero of the poem depicting the tremulous bursting of love's bud, the young husband flushed with ecstasy as he gradually begins to understand the constant state of becoming that true love brings, the husband of years' standing, and the

widower are one and the same, and a man that has or has had
what has been the privilege of only a few.

What could be more graciously understanding or more
tender than the budding love in 'The Generations of Men.'
The humour, the kindliness, the abundant overtones sounding
clearer than the dominant notes of the actual words said by
the girl and boy reflect an enviable inner stability. The poems
in *A Boy's Will* belong essentially to the period of early
marriage while the wonder of love is still an astounding fact.
They express love in divers ways—when the object is present,
absent, or the cause of nostalgic longing. They are ecstatic
in their lyricism, their manly, self-reliant lyricism. 'The
Pasture,' the first poem in *Collected Poems*, although typical, is
frequently misunderstood. It is an unmistakable love poem
with no overt statement of love; the implications fall in the
single line, 'I shan't be gone long—You come too.' Its effect
depends on the correspondence Mr. Frost makes with the
reader. If he creates that correspondence the reader will
naturally inflect the lines to imply the sense of ecstasy and
fulfilment the mere presence of the beloved will inspire at a
moment of such prosy activity as cleaning the spring. She
can transform an insignificant moment into pure gold. The
line typifies Mr. Frost's statement that his aim is to say one
thing and mean another. This quality of unexpressed awareness that bridges an understanding silence better than is possible with words recurs repeatedly; never is it subjected to the
strong unflattering glare of a disillusioned observer. Rather it
gains in strength with the years.[1]

In 'Flower-Gathering,' for example, the word 'love' does
not appear, but could it be more in evidence? It is the same
couple of 'The Pasture.' When the husband starts out in the
morning his wife walks part of the way with him. This itself
ties him more closely to her and makes him sad to go. When

---

[1] I am aware, of course, that this poem has two other possible levels of meaning:
one, a simple descriptive nature poem, and, two, the poet's invitation to the reader
to share with him the pleasures of his poems.

he returns in the evening she meets him in silence, but a silence that leads him to believe that it is her love that silences her. Could the warmth of her greeting be all for him, and not for the flowers that took him from her side for the ages of a day? The diction, the melodies, attest the poet's depth of feeling far better than could rhapsodic outpourings of time-worn words. Even during separation, however, she is not far from his thoughts. He is aware, too—minutely aware—of the phenomena of nature as he sits dreaming against a haycock in the early moonlight; but he is most aware of her who will greet him upon his return ('Waiting'). How much they mean to one another! A similar quality of love is humorously caught in the cinquain 'In Neglect,' the idea of which will receive deeper expression in the later poems:

> They leave us so to the way we took,
> As two in whom they were proved mistaken,
> That we sit sometimes in the wayside nook,
> With mischievous, vagrant, seraphic look,
> And try if we cannot feel forsaken.

It is obvious that Mr. Frost not only thinks of companionship and complete congeniality as prime qualities of love, but that he cannot conceive of love without them. Even the performance of such a necessary farm chore as going for water can assume an ecstatic aura if performed with the beloved. It can become an adventure as deeply stirring as that felt by Paolo and Francesca when reading the story of Lancelot. Here again, however, the love manifests itself by a gaiety of mood that the inexperienced might interpret as indifference. One must understand love to understand the couple that ran as if to meet the dawning moon and then, upon entering the wood, slowed down until each laid on the other a staying hand. The spontaneity of the mutual action is of far greater significance than words could have been, particularly as they stood in the hush they joined to make. Like the shy, sensitive persons that they were, they concealed their love behind light, teasing words; and because they found no release in lofty phrases the passion deepened and enriched them. The poem takes on added significance if we remember the symbolism Frost attaches to the wood. 'Revelation,' in fact, not only gives us a clue to love as it appears in Mr. Frost's poems, it is a key to the poetry in general.

One errs greatly to mistake restraint for coldness; or decorum for lack of passion. Mr. Frost's restraint is the natural reserve one associates with persons with generations of New England ancestry. When such persons are able to give freely they can give abundantly. It is no opening of the sluices to let through a trickle. An Englishman could better appreciate Mr. Frost than the American who linguistically is not a part of the small New England area. 'The Telephone' well illustrates my meaning. A model of restraint, it says far more than could a flood of words. Before the wife will reply to his question if she remembered what she said to him while he was separated from her, she would first know what he thought she had said. From the flower he held by the stalk he thought she had called him by name, or merely called 'Come.' Her reply and his brief answer communicate to the reader the warmth they had themselves experienced.

'The Death of the Hired Man' foreshadows the later poems on love, poems in which love and philosophy blend. Outwardly the poem may be about poor Silas come home to Warren and Mary to die, come to the place where he knew he would be received. He unconsciously sensed that where such love as theirs exists, there kindness must also dwell. The most permanent effect on the reader is the sense of having been a sharer in the richest experience possible to man. When a man can have this thing, the world opens to him as it is impossible for it otherwise to do. Even his attempts to plumb the meaning of life, as in 'West-Running Brook,' take on a richness and profundity when they can be shared and hallowed.

As Mr. Frost is himself aware ('Bond and Free'), it may be
true that love may need something to which to cling, and
that thought has a pair of dauntless wings with which to soar
untrammelled into space. But does thought actually have the
advantage? Does it arrive at an understanding of life that is
impossible through love?

> His gains [thoughts] in heaven are what they are.
> Yet some say love by being thrall
> And simply staying possesses all
> In several beauty that thought fares far
> To find fused in another star.

At another time, and under different conditions, Blake
arrived at a similar conclusion in 'The Clod and the Pebble.'
'Two Look at Two' is his further answer to the question.
Brought to reality from love and forgetfulness by a tumbled
wall with barbed-wire binding, the couple hesitates before
turning back. At that moment a doe looking at them unafraid from behind a spruce passed along the wall as if she
sensed their love as a protecting force; a moment later they
noticed a buck watching them. He also passed them unafraid.
Could the animals have sensed their feeling and they theirs?
Mr. Frost suggests his faith in the power of love in the final
lines:

> Still they stood,
> A great wave from it going over them,
> As if the earth in one unlooked for favor
> Had made them certain earth returned their love.

This power of love cannot be dispelled by years of thought on
the nature of life, and in one of his latest volumes he still looks
upon it as one of the great creative forces ('All Revelation').

As Mr. Frost has grown older he has realized that the
nature of love alters, that the meaning of life constantly
obtrudes itself, preventing the early satisfaction from moments
of pure sensuousness. Just as Yeats' poems reveal a steady

change from youth to age, so, too, do his. The change is not inherent in poems like 'The Death of the Hired Man,' because the couple is essentially preoccupied with other things, but the state of complete understanding at which they had arrived indicates what is to come. He heralds the definite arrival of this moment in 'To Earthward.' In youth 'love at the lips was touch as sweet' as he could bear; in later years pain was necessary to give flavour to joy, and he craved 'the stain of tears, the aftermark of almost too much love.' This pain need not necessarily be harmful; it can be a bringer of strength.

To a man deeply in love with his wife, her death is a tremendous blow. One evidence of this in Mr. Frost is his comparative silence on the subject. In Hardy's case, his wife's death made him vocal because the years had obscured his early feeling. Only four poems in *West-Running Brook* voice Mr. Frost's loss: 'Lodged,' 'A Minor Bird,' 'Bereft,' and 'Tree at My Window.' Read together they give a picture of his benumbment. Quiet, short, simple, they are deeply moving. Typically enough, he reveals his sorrow by analogizing. They are associated with moments in nature: a driving rain, a bird's song, a fierce autumn wind, a tree at his window. In the first he associates himself with the flowers which 'lay lodged' by the storm—'I know how the flowers felt'; in the second he realizes his state by the observation—

> And of course there must be something wrong
> In wanting to silence any song;

in the third he is aware of the necessity of faith—

> Word I was in the house alone
> Somehow must have gotten abroad,
> Word I was in my life alone,
> Word I had no one left but God;

and in the fourth he indicates the extent of his grief—

> You have seen me when I was taken and swept
> And all but lost.

'The Onset' and 'An Old Man's Winter Night' present a similar sense of desolation following the loss of the beloved. It is perhaps needless to add that the experience is no less real even if it is only an intensely imagined one. I mention this because 'Bereft' was an early-conceived poem.

A man who has been granted the riches of love never turns from it even when it is no longer for him. He experiences a vicarious pleasure whenever he finds it to exist, and his imagination gives him wings by which he can continue its enjoyment. In retrospect, too, he can relive unforgettable moments, like that one, for example, when years before, during his sojourn in England, he and his wife found themselves experiencing a miracle of nature. The moon shining through the air heavy with dew made a rainbow about them that, instead of moving as they moved, closed a circle, while they

> . . . stood in it softly circled round
> From all division time or foe can bring
> In a relation of elected friends.

'Elected friends' describes their relationship.

In two short poems addressed to a young couple he conveys all that love can mean to them as in the past it had meant to him. Their speed is not to keep up with the 'rush of everything to waste,' but to enable them in the midst of hurry and bustle to 'have the power of standing still.' With such power, he adds,

> Two such as you with such a master speed
> Cannot be parted nor be swept away
> From one another once you are agreed
> That life is only life for evermore
> Together wing to wing and oar to oar.
>   'The Master Speed'

'Moon Compasses' (by means of a sustained simile) expresses differently the exalting power of love.

Even when one might least suspect, this engulfing power assumes the ascendancy in Frost's consciousness. A view from his sleeper window of a small Utah town takes him past the light, that because of the trees only seems to flicker, to the couple in the house where the light burns steadily. Then faith in one another is free of fear, and because of that they cannot fear life. They have the added protection of neighbours whose lives are similar to theirs.

The captured reader naturally asks how it is that by the power of suggestion Mr. Frost has been able to evoke a correspondence greater than he could have done had he resorted to overt statement. Actually, of course, it is his suggestiveness that frees the imagination. If the reader is too young or too unfortunate never to have experienced the transcendent joy of love on Mr. Frost's plane, the poetry will carry little meaning. Even if he has not experienced the emotion in a similar relationship, he may still experience it vicariously, particularly if he is sensitive to the beauty of the physical world. This is because Mr. Frost draws so largely from his own passionate observation of the natural world to illustrate this not less tangible but less easily described experience. Is it love that sheds the passionate radiance over the scene, or is it the beauty of the scene that stimulates a correspondence in human emotions? Probably neither. Both are rich because of the richness of spirit that he takes to each experience. There is the same purity, the same sensuous capacity, the same sensitivity, the same power that enables him to 'climb back up a stream of radiance to the sky.'

Mr. Frost is aware that love as he has experienced it is uncommon and often takes more prosaic forms. The un-initiated would probably miss the *rapport* between the man and wife in *The Masque of Mercy*. Some persons, too, simply lack the imagination necessary to love. Perhaps that was the case with the girl in 'The Subverted Flower.' There can be no meeting and fusing of the spirit when one or both are deficient. Love for such persons necessarily will be on a lower plane, on a more physical basis, without the wings of aspiration. It may be, of course, that the nearness of the world stifled the delicate shoots. *North of Boston* contains several poems suggesting that this might have been the case, and 'The Investment,' from *West-Running Brook*, implies that no outward adjustments can recompense for its absence. The person who understands the nature of love realizes that no change of physical background can ever supply its lack. In the country north of Boston the opportunities for running away are more restricted than in the small and large cities. The only means of escape is through madness in mild or severe forms. It is through those forms that many of the poet's characters find the only freedom they can ever know.

I have here spoken of what Mr. Frost does. To see how he does it, the reader must turn to the poems themselves. In a later section I have suggested the technical means by which he spreads a radiance over all things. The reader must make his own application of those technical means to the poems, remembering always, however, that beneath everything is a rich, comprehensive, and warmly passionate nature so disciplined in the art of expression that communication of the qualities of soul is possible.

II. CRITIC OF LIFE

In Mr. Frost's earlier work, as I have already suggested in the preceding section on his treatment of love, the sensuous elements dominate but never obscure the rational; in mid-career the sensuous and rational are about evenly distributed; in his latest work the purely rational gain a decided ascendancy. The emphasis changes, that is all. Both the sensuous and rational elements must be present at the beginning and persist to the end. Perhaps it would be truer to say that the sensuous elements in the later lyrics become subtler, are less of the surface than of the deeps. Since Mr. Frost brought his wares late to market this should be so. A man who publishes his first volume at thirty-seven must bring more than pure sensuousness if he expects to live. Mr. Frost is most sensuous in those subjects where persons are generally so, in their attitude toward love and nature. We have already examined 'love's alternations, joy and grief' and the unique radiance he has cast on the understanding love possible between man and wife. The following section will consider his attitude toward nature —'the weather's alternations, Summer and Winter, Our age-long theme.' Our present task is to consider the more purely intellectual aspects of the poet.

Mr. Frost has hammered out his own philosophy, the rationale of which can be simply expressed. His poetry makes possible the route by which he arrived at the ideas expressed in *Steeple Bush* and *The Masque of Mercy*, a route along which certain landmarks such as 'New Hampshire,' 'Build Soil,' 'The Lesson for To-day' stand out more boldly than others.

Mr. Frost early realized that he who would come to a just view of life cannot be for ever 'busy,' nor can he maintain an undeviating point of view. He must be able to see the microcosm in the macrocosm and the macrocosm in the microcosm. He recognized the importance of and the necessity for contemplation before he could expect a permanent settlement of his own problems. He looked for no basic change in the fundamental tenets of his faith, only a greater surety of their truth ('Into My Own'). The purely contemplative life away from the world, however, was not enough. He knew that man needs man; not, however, as a means of escaping from himself, but as food for his thinking. He needs to observe him in his daily activities, he needs to ponder the meaning of death, and, even more, the aims of life. When these do not suffice, he needs to turn to a bruised plant, the earth, or to look into the 'crater' of an ant ('The Vantage Point'). He needs the perspective possible through a telescope and the accuracy of facts possible through a microscope, and the tolerance that sometimes comes from politics. Mr. Frost's vision is not restricted to one plane. He has looked up, into, and across others. Because he based his thinking on facts—'the fact is the sweetest dream that labour knows'—he has attained unto wisdom.

Mr. Frost has little use for sententious philosophizing: he is too profound, too wise, for that. His New England shyness and reticence may forbid his dressing his thoughts in formal robes, but he is none the less anxious that those thoughts be grasped. He gives us a clue in 'Revelation':

> We make ourselves a place apart
> Behind light words that tease and flout,
> But oh, the agitated heart
> Till someone find us really out.

Poems that 'tease and flout' are particularly frequent in his last four volumes. He realized, too, that to arrive at any fundamental truth he had to bring the 'maturest, the longest-saved-up, raciest, localest' thoughts he had 'strength of reserve' in himself to bring ('Build Soil'). One of the earliest of the poet's direct expositions of his philosophy occurs in 'The Trial By Existence,' the very rhythms of which reflect his youthful confidence, one that even in a poet less tightly muscled than Mr. Frost could not easily lead to later disillusionment. He suggests that men are really of an angelic breed, although ironically, they have lost that memory; and that life, too, is a choice. All that we are, all that we may become, stems from our own volition:

> 'Tis the essence of life here,
> Though we choose greatly, still to lack
> The lasting memory at all clear,
> That life has for us on the wrack
> Nothing but what we somehow chose.

Armed with such a philosophy one rids oneself of the tempta-

E

tion to self-pity. A Frostian touch breathes through the poem
in his suggestion that the simple life sounds better in heaven
than it does on earth—

> The tale of earth's unhonored things
> Sounds nobler there than 'neath the sun.

A second bolstering thought is one theme of 'The Tuft of
Flowers'—the joy that springs from the conviction that we
are not alone in our interests—'that men work together . . .
whether they work together or apart.' Is this a conscious
denial of Robinson's idea that each man has a darkening hill to
climb, and alone—the theme of 'A Man Against the Sky' and
'An Evening At Shannon's'?

Armed with the conviction that our lives depend on our
own choices and that somewhere there is someone who
shares our loves and enthusiasms, a man must face life with
optimism. Not only must he remain open-minded, but he
must entertain the strong conviction that a person of healthy
sanity will do his utmost to extract from his life on earth the
best that earth can offer. He will take life as he finds it here
and not concern himself with the hereafter. This is not to
suggest that Mr. Frost is a hedonistic poet in the manner of
Simonides of Amorgos or Mimnerus of Colophon; he is rather
in the Homeric tradition recognizing that the very shortness of
our lives on earth demands that we devote our time to the
improvement of our souls. In his later years Mr. Frost shares
Hardy's convictions of the nature of the government of the
world. Whereas Hardy's convictions make him gloomy,
Frost wears his with humour, lightness, and affirmation.

Mr. Frost is strongly traditional; although he has little use
for tradition as such. He is conservative in the finest sense of
the word with a strong mixture of Yankee shrewdness and
common sense. Each generation, he believes, must re-
examine the customs by which it lives and discard the out-
moded ones in order to keep vital those which are sound

('Mending Wall,' and several epigrams in *Steeple Bush*). Not to do this keeps man from progressing; holds him, in fact, to the mental habits of a dweller in the stone age. This does not mean, however, that the poet believes a person should seize on every new and untried idea that passes by, or that he should discard a belief that happens to be out of fashion. Quite the contrary. When you are convinced that you have in your grasp an idea that is basically sound, hold to it with all your powers. Frost shares the convictions of the widow of 'The Black Cottage,' that charming, independent old lady who insisted on others' right of independence:

> She valued the considerate neglect
> She had at some cost taught them after years.

This woman believed in strict equality, recognized no racial discrimination, because, she asks,

> . . . how could they be made so very unlike
> By the same hand working in the same stuff?

She possessed true innocence, a quality which, like Milton, Mr. Frost believes to be a powerful force.

> Strange how innocence gets its own way.
> I shouldn't be surprised if in this world
> It were the force that would at last prevail.

And, he suggests (because there are fashions in truth as there are fashions in all things), was she not right in not paying too much heed to many of the latter-day ideas. Truth, after all, is what people want it to be. This raises, however, a more pertinent question at the solution of which Mr. Frost never actually arrives, although he poses the question both early and late ('The Black Cottage,' 'To a Thinker'). Perhaps no one could arrive at a satisfactory conclusion. Is there such a thing as progress or is there only change? Is progress no more than a swing of the pendulum in the opposite direction? Hardy likewise asked the same questions. To have asked them is

meritorious even when no satisfactory answer is forth-
coming, prevents smug complacency, and induces true
humility.

The important thing, says the poet under other circumstances, 'is the ideals' ('The Generations of Men'). Each must
choose for himself; a thing neither easy, nor conclusive.
Another choice, greater riches ('The Road Not Taken')?
At least the necessity for choice and its accompanying doubts
need tolerance. No choice, however, springs from a definite
beginning nor leads to a like conclusion. Life is always a
series of middles. Or, as Joe's wife tells him:

> 'You're searching, Joe,
> For things that don't exist; I mean beginnings.
> Ends and beginnings—there are no such things.
> There are only middles.'

And later,

> New is a word for fools in towns who think
> Style upon style in dress and thought at last
> Must get somewhere.
>
> 'In the Home Stretch'

The seeming purposelessness of the poet's life—his willingness to 'wander out of beaten ways *half-looking* for the orchid
Calypso'—differs markedly from the obvious purposefulness
of the telegraph pole.

The reader should guard against a misinterpretation. A
satisfactory answer depends first of all on the answer to what
the purpose of life is. Is it to be, or to do? By his insistence
on his right to be, Mr. Frost actually accomplishes more than
they who insist that the only aim in life is to do. But he
never confuses 'being' with mere 'vegetating.' Those periods
when he most seems to concentrate on being—when he lies
fallow—are responsible for the later richness of the crops.
The man of action is apt to reduce his own effectiveness by
not recognizing the paramount importance of these fallow

periods. The gospel of work for the sake of work has done as much, or more, harm as good.

Even on this matter of work, however, Mr. Frost's ideas are worth heeding. His ideas are homely ones, it is true, but they are none the less too often disregarded. A man should engage in that form of work that brings him happiness and satisfaction. It should be work that were the necessity of the profit motive removed he would still be content to do. The idea, first suggested in 'The Gum-Gatherer,' is more fully crystallized in 'Two Tramps in Mudtime.'

> But yield who will to their separation,
> My object in living is to unite
> My avocation and my vocation.
> As my two eyes make one in sight.
> Only where love and need are one,
> And the work is play for mortal stakes,
> Is the deed ever really done
> For Heaven and the future's sakes.

The difference of treatment in the two poems typifies the change everywhere manifest in the texture of the work as the intellectual element gains the ascendancy over pure sensuousness.

No one should minimize the sensuous elements of 'Two Tramps in Mudtime,' however lightly they may be expressed. Each stanza has a richness of its own that contributes to the general effect. The poet leaves nothing to chance in the interpretation he wishes from his reader. He canalizes his thought by qualifying exposition. By means of this greater control, he intensifies the impact, making it comparable to that achieved by the greater sensuousness of the earlier poems. The point at which the earlier method fuses with the later finds perfect expression in 'The Road Not Taken.'

A seeming random statement in 'Snow' furnishes a clue to the manner in which Mr. Frost has developed. It is the clue to every person's development; it is the essence of maturity. The mind must first be able to grasp before the eye can see, the ear hear, the palate taste, the nose smell, and the tactile senses feel. We constantly question our inability to see the obvious, forgetting that the obvious is only so in retrospect. Whether it be a word or image in a poem that has passed us by, or the face of close acquaintance that eluded us until we attempted to model it, or a phrase of music that had to be pointed out to us, it is all the same. Things, says Frost through Meserve ('Snow'), must many times 'expect to come in front of us.' 'One of the lies,' he continues,

> . . . would make it out that nothing
> Ever presents itself before us twice.
> Where would we be at last if that were so?
> Our very life depends on everything's
> Recurring till we answer from within.
> The thousandth time may prove the charm.

But Meserve's thinking did not stop there. He contemplated what a thing is man; how seemingly insufficient when compared with the birds to whom he would not willingly be counted less if resolute will and determination could prevent it.

Just as the intellectual elements in the poems increase as Mr. Frost approaches and passes fifty, so do the purely sensuous elements become more controlled. They never wholly disappear and often assert themselves with striking force even in *Steeple Bush*. He realized in 'New Hampshire,' 'The Star Splitter,' and 'Wild Grapes' that his heart would always loom large in his work. He loves his people, and as he himself says, 'To be social is to be forgiving.' The generalizations he makes about life have validity because they arise from his own observations, suffering, and exquisite balance. Being a person sensitive to the life about him he knows he shall never lack the pain to keep him awake; because he had not learned to let go with the heart, and saw no need for so doing. Heart, head, and all the other qualities of humour, nature, colloquialism, which we associate with Mr. Frost, find typical fusion in his most typical poem, 'New Hampshire'; typical but not his most successful.

This quality of heart and his constant search for the truth that emerges only with a catholicity of experience frequently endow the least promising of themes with richness and wisdom. The striking change of men from high estate to low, from riches to poverty, are as familiar as they are obvious. Mr. Frost has seen the deep sub-surface declensions not apparent to others. The fall may be as steep beneath an outward stability as in those where the change is obvious. The length of the radius is not so important as the angle of the arc. 'You *can* come down from everything to nothing,' says the poet, revealing, too, that perhaps the greatest declension can happen outside the vision of the multitude. If in youth the gift of foresight had permitted us to see what our end would be, how many of us would have had the courage 'to make so free and kick up in folks' faces'? Some might have had, 'but it doesn't seem as if,' says the pauper witch of Grafton ('The Pauper Witch of Grafton'). If we fail, and can clearly see wherein and why we have failed, we have achieved more than those who have stumbled blindly and unwittingly into success, into what the poet calls 'life's victories of doubt,' victories that need endless talk before they come into *any* focus, not necessarily a sharply defined one ('An Empty Threat'). And if the result is death? Well, in his characteristic indirect way he mentions that there is no immortality as people usually think of it ('In a Disused Graveyard,' 'A Steeple on the House'). Expressed differently, he wishes to meet Death still desirous of discovering the 'knowledge beyond the bounds of life' ('Misgiving').

This constant insistence on the necessity for vibrant awareness of the immediacy of life here and now and his unwillingness to escape from life constitute much of Mr. Frost's strength. Sensuous beauty may be enough in youth—a kiss from the beloved, a touch of a rose petal on the hand—but maturity (if it is to continue to grow) takes its nourishment from sterner stuff. Mere pain will not do; it also needs the struggle:

> The hurt is not enough
> I long for weight and strength
> To feel the earth as rough
> To all my length.
>
> 'To Earthward'

Possessed of the determination, nothing can keep us from the goal 'we have it hidden in us to attain' ('On a Tree Fallen Across the Road'). Above all, however, we must accept the theme of a poem rich in its overtones with the several levels of meaning:

> Let the night be too dark for me to see
> Into the future. Let what will be, be.
>
> 'Acceptance'

Because, as he has elsewhere said, 'the Cross, the Crown, the Scales' may 'as well have been the Sword' for all the good they have done ('The Peaceful Shepherd'). In spite of his occasional dark moods, however, more sharply etched in *A Witness Tree* and *Steeple Bush*, the poet's acceptance, his objectivity, his fine sense of proportion thwart despair ('Acceptance,' 'In Time of Cloudburst'). Notwithstanding, too, the infinite details which, in a short view of life, negate the idea of man's improvement, he can see that, actually, life is always 'raising a little, sending up a little,' that the spirit flies farther than any target, that through thought man achieves his true freedom ('West-Running Brook,' 'A Soldier,' 'Sand Dunes,' 'Immigrants,' 'Riders,' etc.).

What is it, he asks in a later poem,

> What comes over a man, is it soul or mind—
> That to no limits and bounds he can stay confined?

.   .   .   .   .

Why is his nature forever so hard to teach
That though there is no fixed line between wrong and
        right,
There are roughly zones whose laws must be obeyed.
                    'There are Roughly Zones'

To see this, man must possess true humility, a quality everywhere manifest in Mr. Frost's poetry, but given metaphorical
expression in 'Dust In the Eyes' and 'On Being Idolized.'
Thought is not the mere agreement with this or that tradition,
or this or that particular thinker; it is not being simply
'intermental'; thought springs from the shocks and changes
we everywhere encounter and the constructive use we make of
those phenomena ('Build Soil,' 'On Looking Up By Chance
etc.,' 'The Bear,' 'The Courage To Be New'). It is closely
allied, too, with self-discipline or self-control, the possession
of which gives man the reserve power which he can use
for the common good ('Two Tramps in Mudtime'). Man's
thought must not, however, lead him to 'downward comparison.' He must look out and up if he is to be true man
'but little lower than the gods and angels.' 'Once comparisons
were yielded downward,' he says,

    Once we began to see our images
    Reflected in the mud and even dust
    'Twas disillusion upon disillusion,
    We were lost piecemeal to the animals
    Like people thrown out to delay the wolves.
    Nothing but fallibility was left us,
    And this day's work made even that seem doubtful.
                    'The White-tailed Hornet'

On the other hand, we should not let ourselves become
'sick with space' and minimize ourselves. Even this, however,
is better than no thought, a state into which many persons
escape by way of the movies ('A Roadside Stand'). He is
particularly provoked by the farmers living about him who

fail to see the richness of their possessions and elevate the
poor materialism of the city-dweller into something devoutly
to be wished for. The secret of life, he suggests many times
both directly and indirectly, is 'knowing what to do with
things that count' ('The Figure in the Doorway,' 'At Wood-
ward's Gardens').

Like every well-adjusted person, Mr. Frost is not troubled
by death, is not perturbed by the vast unknown reaches of
the universe, nor by the nature of the hereafter if there be
one, nor about the nature or power of God. His fear is pro-
ductive; it is only fear for what he may have failed to do,
the courage he may have failed to manifest ('Desert Places').
Lost is the person who tries to live on memories; he must
rely only on himself, must not let himself be pigeon-holed
or too easily classified ('Provide Provide,' 'Precaution'). If in
The Masque of Reason and *The Masque of Mercy* he finally suggests
answers to universal questions that seem unsatisfactory to
many, we must recognize that at least he has journeyed.
Strangely enough the answers, already several times hinted at
in *The Witness Tree* and *Steeple Bush*, are not so different from
some of the answers expressed by Hardy in *The Dynasts*. Mr.
Frost found no easy answer to his questions on the nature of
life or the world. It is something that love is one of the
greatest forces. It is something, too, that one day of boundless
happiness can atone for a number of less fortunate days which
were not so fair. Actually, however, man cannot live in the
present—it 'is too much for the senses, too crowding, too
confusing, too present to imagine.' He can live only in the
future, and, even more so, in the past. But we should not
worry. 'Soon it is neither here nor there whether time's
rewards are fair or unfair.'[1]

The answers to the questions Mr. Frost has asked over the
years bring him the calm acceptance of life for which he has

[1] 'All Revelation,' 'Happiness Makes Up in Height, etc,' 'Carpe Diem,' 'The Discovery of the Madeiras.'

striven. Society may not have been able to think things out, but he has. He has found out, to borrow the words of one of his characters, that

> . . . the discipline man needed most
> Was to learn his submission to unreason;
> And that for man's own sake as well as mine,
> So he won't find it hard to take his orders
> From his inferiors in intelligence
> In peace and war—especially in war.
>
> *The Masque of Reason*, p. 12

He has learned, too, to accept injustice and the assurance that the fundamental truths never change. It is Mr. Frost's attitude toward the problem of justice and injustice in *The Masque of Mercy* that would repel many of the younger generation who have turned to Catholicism as an answer to their problems. The outward sense of relaxation in his latest work should not blind the reader to the richness of the thought or the felicity of expression. Mr. Frost is not misled by the philosophic jargon that reveals nothing. The chances are, he says,

> . . . When there's so much pretence
> Of metaphysical profundity
> The obscurity's a fraud to cover nothing.
>
> *The Masque of Reason*, p. 14

There is no pretence at metaphysical profundity in Mr. Frost's poetry. There is only the profundity that springs from his wrestlings with the problems of life. If his answers differ little or only slightly from those found by others to the same questions, their validity is no less. The restatement of these answers in terms that enrich their communication is important. We have not only the ideas themselves, but Mr. Frost's passionate expression of his conviction and joy in those truths, in language that inspires the reader of his poems with a renewed conviction of the timelessness of basic ethical truths. Few modern poets have with so little ostentation assimilated the findings of science.

III. POET OF NATURE

Mr. Frost's use of sustained metaphor for his avowed purpose of saying one thing and meaning another has enabled him to achieve a subtlety of expression and a richness of meaning not possible through direct statement. In this he resembles the early allegorists who created an instrument for the communication of psychological states otherwise impossible in their time. Nowhere does this characteristic become more manifest than in his so-called nature poems. I would not give the impression that Mr. Frost always uses nature for this, or for any single purpose. Nature serves him in many ways and we must look at each individually. To speak of Mr. Frost as a nature poet is so broad as to be meaningless. Certain poems, it is true, seem to be almost pure description of natural phenomena, yet the poet arouses his reader to a state of correspondence which transforms the final impression of the poem into a glimpse into the poet's soul, a starting of warmth between friends who have shared an aesthetic pleasure, a confirmation of the conviction that 'men work together.'

The symbolic strain in the poetry is manifest in the brief descriptive passages Mr. Frost subjoined to the titles in *A Boy's Will* and *A Further Range*, as well as in the grouping of poems in other volumes. Since in the *Collected Poems* he almost wholly omits to hint how the poems should be interpreted let us turn for a moment to some of the poems and their interpretative comments in *A Boy's Will*. An obvious interpretation of 'Into My Own' is that the poet finds his greatest fulfilment in intimate contact with nature, especially the woods. The poet is more specific in his statement of its autobiographic implications: 'The youth is persuaded that he will be rather more than less himself for having forsworn the world.' To 'Ghost House' he added 'He is happy in his own choosing'; to 'Storm Fear,' 'He is afraid of his own isolation.' The second section of the volume contains poems depicting the youth's resolution to become intelligible to himself, to find out what he thinks about the soul, about love, fellowship, and death, about the art of poetry, and about science. The third section contains poems dealing with his acceptance. Now all of these ideas are implicit in the poems and the careful reader has no difficulty in seeing that the poems are specific on these matters. But even were the reader to miss this more intimate communication, the poems are still valuable for a less symbolic meaning. 'Ghost House,' for example, is an excellent vignette the power of which derives from the poet's selection of only the most essential details vivified by an apt epithet. In his imagination he dwells in a lonely house long since vanished where the wild raspberries grow over the cellar walls, where the grape-vines shield the ruined fences, and the footpath has disappeared under returned vegetation. One could enumerate additional details, even the dead whose head-stones are now moss-covered. In spite of the loneliness of this abandoned spot, he says, 'in view of how many things, as sweet companions as might be had.'

Only one conclusion is possible from a comparison of the poem with his statement about it. The intellectual idea behind the poem is less important than the spiritual communion he establishes with the reader. This accounts for the importance Mr. Frost attaches to 'colour' in his poems rather than to an obvious 'form.' But I would not be understood to say that Mr. Frost lacks form; rather he stresses the importance of colour in form. It is perhaps futile to analogize on poets so different as Hardy and Frost. But since I turned from a long period of study of Hardy to a similiar one of Mr. Frost certain differences became even more glaring than otherwise might have been possible. It is relatively easy to paraphrase a poem of Hardy's without a complete loss. Mr. Frost is so completely the poet that the moment one attempts to paraphrase, nothing is left. Hardy is a poet of the head; his subject-matter is the result of intellectual observation. Mr. Frost has looked long enough at his subject to have turned intellectual knowledge into wisdom.

But to return to the subject of nature in the poems. We must perforce recognize a changing attitude in the poet toward the subject as he grows older; but the changes occur within the orbit of love and profound knowledge. No season is without its fascination for him. The locale is chiefly New England simply because that is the part of the country he knows intimately. He does not select his details because they are typically and solely New England, but because they are important in themselves, and would be anywhere. He writes about what he knows, and few persons know their own district as well as Mr. Frost knows his New Hampshire and Vermont. I stress this to avoid Mr. Frost's being considered a regional poet. Nothing, as I have earlier suggested, is farther from fact. He has used regional details to bolster and illumine general universal truths. Just as he looks at the folk north of Boston as typical representatives of a certain type of humanity, so, too, does he look at the countryside. His underlying deep humanity enables him to see the beauty in ugliness and desolation as symbolic of man's processes. The quality of soul and understanding that he brings to bear on a subject which would to many persons be trivial transforms it into one of significance. In several of his shorter poems on nature, for example, the reader quickens to their richness and beauty not because of the extraordinary quality of the incidents in the poem, but because of the extraordinary character and vision of the man who can see significance in those incidents.

In these poems, as in those on love, the poet demands much from his reader. He relies on him to bring a quality of soul (or correspondence) to the poems that will permit him to see what he has himself seen. For this reason, in spite of Mr. Frost's general acclaim, he can never be a truly popular poet with the crowd. He is too much the natural aristocrat for that. The scene can be one of spring, summer, autumn, or winter, joyous or melancholy, evocative of other poetry or intensely original. Only in the earliest work, however, and in his latest when he is poking fun at the followers of Mr. Eliot is one obviously conscious of other poetry. 'A Prayer in Spring,' for example, starts the memory of Rupert Brooke with its 'like nothing else by day, like ghosts by night.'

The outstanding characteristics of these nature poems, however, and it is also as true of the later poems where nature joins hands with religion, philosophy, or political thinking, is the reportorial quality of the poet. His facts are easily verifiable, but until Mr. Frost pointed them out one was unaware of them. The details of 'My November Guest,' 'A Late Walk,' and 'Now Close the Windows' are sufficient to induce in the reader the memory of similar experiences, even though it be of vividly felt imaginative experiences. 'Stars' does the same for winter, and 'To the Thawing Wind,' 'A Prayer in Spring,' for spring, and 'Waiting' for summer. The deepest appeal of all the poems is not in what the poet has said but, as it should be, in his way of saying it.

I have mentioned the importance of emotional colour in Mr. Frost's poetry. Any one of several poems in *A Boy's Will* would illustrate what I mean, but let us look at the richly suggestive 'October':

> O hushed October morning mild,
> Thy leaves have ripened to the fall;
> To-morrow's wind, if it be wild,
> Should waste them all.
> The crows above the forest call;
> To-morrow they may form and go.

O hushed October morning mild,
Begin the hours of this day slow.
Make the day seem to us less brief.
Hearts not averse to being beguiled,
Beguile us in the way you know.
Release one leaf at break of day;
At noon release another leaf;
One from our trees, one far away.
Retard the sun with gentle mist;
Enchant the land with amethyst.
Slow, slow!
For the grapes' sake, if they were all
Whose leaves already are burnt with frost,
Whose clustered fruit must else be lost—
For the grapes' sake along the wall.

Apart from the rather obvious use of liquids, back vowels, and end-stopped lines to pace the mood, the poet enhances the communication by making the poem a directive to October of what she should do, rather than a simple statement of what is happening. The calling up of the way of past Octobers lends richness to the present one. The opening lines constitute a report of the setting, heightened by the apprehensiveness induced by the third, fourth, fifth, and sixth. The 'thy' of line two instead of 'your' is consciously selected for its effect. The image of the migratory crows furnishes an ominous sign. With the seventh the supplication begins. Line eleven joins the present with the past, and we are ready for specific details. The subtle music of lines twelve to fourteen is partially achieved by the repetition of 'release,' 'leaf,' and 'one,' partially by the delicate nuance of the prosodic structure.

> Release one leaf at break of day
> At noon release another leaf;
> One from our trees, one far away.

The movement steadily slows down until we come to 'Slow, slow!' The mood shifts, becomes lighter in quality, although the general sensuousness of the passage intensifies.

The reader should expect to find that as the poet leaves the sensuous period of youth the more purely sensuous revelry in nature should lessen. This is not to say that the poet himself will find a less sensuous ecstasy in nature—he may experience a greater one and probably does—but for the purposes of poetry he exercises greater control over it. His palette will be cooler, the tones slightly greyed. True though it be that a man remains the perpetual boy when in contact with nature, he is often reluctant to admit it. Inhibition can be a besetting sin. But in his pronouncements to the world a change takes place. After all, an artist cannot sing endless variations on one theme, and the world expects more and more criticism of life as the artist ages.

'The Death of the Hired Man' reveals a new use of nature to fortify a poem. In fact, two passages in this poem do much to suffuse the whole with the love that surely exists between Mary and Warren. The first follows the characterization of Silas—

> 'And nothing to look backward to with pride,
>   And nothing to look forward to with hope,
> So now and never any different.'

It provides the change of mood necessary for the effectiveness of Mr. Frost's memorable description of home as the 'place where, when you have to go there, they have to take you in.' The passage is simple and straightforward, but the diction is incontrovertibly right for the purity of the idyll—

> Part of a moon was falling down the west,
> Dragging the whole sky with it to the hills.
> Its light poured softly in her lap. She saw it
> And spread her apron to it. She put out her hand

F

Among the harp-like morning-glory strings,
Taut with the dew from garden bed to eaves,
As if she played unheard some tenderness
That wrought on him beside her in the night.

The second passage, occurring near the end of the poem, performs a similar function and so works on the reader that the impact of the final lines is forceful.

Although it is not always so easy to separate the nature passages in poems on basically different subjects, they occur when the reader least suspects them. Often it is only a line, but one so pregnant with truth that the reader is startled into an awareness of the rich treasury of observed natural phenomena Mr. Frost has at his command. In poems like 'Birches' and 'Mending Wall,' for example, the precision and range of his observation linked with his analogizing power constantly excite the reader.

Mr. Frost, like Wordsworth, has no need of the grander aspects of nature to arouse his demon. Nor does he feel any more than does Wordsworth that he must evoke from the meanest flower that blows a thought that lies too deep for tears. His approach to nature is akin to that of a seventeenth-century Dutch painter to his subject. He loves the minutiae with such a passionate love that he can lavish his attention on the object itself and not on a moral issuing from that object. This quality is evident in the early poetry, but becomes increasingly so in subsequent volumes. As he says in 'Hyla Brook,' 'We love the things we love for what they are'; and as he reveals in 'Stopping by Woods on a Snowy Evening,' love can transcend the power of words to convey it, however felicitously those words may be chosen. He admirably illustrates the truth that any object, however small or seemingly unimportant in itself, can become important according to the quality of spirit the beholder takes to the object. What Wordsworth saw in the English countryside, particularly in the Lake District, Mr. Frost has seen in America, particularly New England.

Even in the poems with a subject less tangibly related to the lives of people, one never escapes from reality. He might, it is true, escape momentarily from his immediate surroundings, but he escapes into a greater reality from which vantage point the world never again is quite the same to him. Never again can he walk through the woods or over fields without the consciousness that he is missing something, and that chief something will be the awareness of the absence of a comprehensive and comprehending soul.

Mr. Frost is in many ways a naturalist's poet. He sees nature with a trained eye and is able, if need be, to call a flower by its botanical name—the *cyprepedium reginae*, for example. He has the scientist's patience to search far and wide for a rare specimen and he is sufficiently familiar with the habits of the Ram's Horn to know that near it one probably will find a Yellow Lady's Slipper. The careful observation of nature used with dramatic effect in 'The Self-Seeker' to heighten Willis's tragedy repeatedly reveals itself in the poems, often with quieter effect.

Mr. Frost, however, transcends the pure naturalist. He not only sees what a naturalist would see, but the quality of his analogizing is such that what a naturalist would present as a dull report, springs to life under his hand. Nowhere is Mr. Frost more surely the poet than in these so frequent moments. He is, too, a most disarming poet. Hardy might say that the art he loved best was the art that concealed art, and yet the joints in his work are often visible. Mr. Frost so perfectly conceals the greatness of his art that some insensible persons deny him the possession of any art at all.

Economy is, of course, an important quality for any artist. He must carefully prevent the weakening of his effect by the obtrusion of irrelevant details. Naturally, Mr. Frost is not always successful, but he is a severe enough critic of his work to hold the failures to the barest minimum. I know of the collected work of no poet of recent decades that contains so little dross. The poems which fail to spring to life often fail from too great an economy rather than from too little. The poet has not given himself time to make the reader feel as he has felt. Over and over again, however, I have discovered the reader to be at fault, not Mr. Frost. Economy is apparent in his treatment of nature.

Again, with a full consciousness of their differences, I shall compare Mr. Frost to Wordsworth. Their methods of portraiture are similar. An artist is aware that once he has the general form of the head, if he can catch the eyes of his subject his portrait will be successful. Next in importance is the mouth. The other details are relatively insignificant, and two features that receive the least attention—and are therefore the most stylized feature of an artist's work—are the ears and hands. Mr. Frost, like Wordsworth, works with nature as an artist works on a portrait. He selects the most important characteristics—those that will control the imagination of the reader—and pays little attention to the rest. He does not limit the suggestiveness of his communication by unnecessary detail. He does not worry his subject or arouse a nervous irritability in his reader. He gives enough leeway for the reader to read into the poem, within bounds, what his experience permits him. The universally admired 'The Road Not Taken' well illustrates what I mean. The subject is a familiar one. Which of two roads shall we choose, and having chosen, what would the one not taken have offered to us? Lord Dunsany in *If*, O. Henry in several stories, and others have posed the same question. Unless we remember, however, that the woods are a symbol for the realm of the poet's spirit ('Into My Own'), we shall miss the greater significance of the poem. Momentarily let us forgo this symbolic meaning and look at it as typical of his nature-painting.

He does not pile detail on detail to make us aware of the

autumnal scene. He speaks of the 'yellow wood' and of the two roads that

> . . . both that morning equally lay
> In leaves no step had trodden black.

That it is early autumn is implicit in the statement that both roads were 'grassy and wanted wear.' They were not wholly deserted nor were they a common thoroughfare—'the passing there had worn them really about the same.' We recreate the scene for ourselves from these few but significant details. From the recreated scene we can then reconstitute the degree of intensity of the problem that had confronted the poet. 'Stopping by Woods on a Snowy Evening' is even more economical in its details. Beside the sound of the harness bells as the horse shakes himself

> The only other sound's the sweep
> Of easy wind and downy flake.

In 'easy' and 'downy' he has fixed the quality of the evening.

Mr. Frost is not an apostle of the picturesque in nature nor of its static quality. His nature descriptions have what can best be described as a linear or fluid quality, by which I imply the sense of movement. They are pictures by an artist walking, observing as he walks, rather than by an artist who has set up his easel to fix on his canvas the details of one spot. It is quite possibly from this habit of observation that his selection of details is appropriate to and effective with the reader. Because he, too, has generally observed nature while walking rather than while reclining on his elbows on the ground. In such a position he will study the habits of the ants, observe the pistils in a flower, and tend to botanize if he has any fundamental knowledge of how to do so. Mr. Frost has looked at nature from this close point of view, and it is this knowledge that is transferred to the fluid observation through the media of accurate epithets. On my walks through the Michigan woods of beech, birch, and hemlock it is lines from Mr. Frost's poetry that most often involuntarily spring to mind. When these come, my pace slackens and I see details rather than mere mass, then I realize that I had not observed 'the form and colour of leaves I had trodden on and mired.' 'The Leaf Treader' is typical of Mr. Frost's middle period.

With the passing years he has depended less and less on nature for his subject-matter. As his knowledge of mankind has increased, and as the mass of observations has mounted he has increasingly tended to deduce generalizations, to philosophize. In his latest years he has become predominantly political. This does not mean, of course, that he has abandoned nature. It still affords him a refuge from the 'busyness' of man. It still provides him with a communing spot for his soul, a place from which he can repair the damages to his perspective that too close contact with man eventually brings.

Adequately to grasp the reaches of Mr. Frost's thought, one must understand his use of nature as metaphor. In the early work his images are drawn largely from the woods. The woods represent his own inner nature and his withdrawal into them typifies his examination of himself. It is necessary, he repeats over and over, that a person must withdraw himself from the activities of life that absorb so large a part of one's time and make experiences from the sensations accompanying these activities. In his middle years references to the woods are less frequent. In his latest collection of lyrics, *Steeple Bush*, the metaphors from the woods have almost wholly given way to those drawn from the stars. The poet has turned from the problems of the personal to those of the universal and abstract. No modern poet has made the transition with more graciousness, because no one else possesses in such large measure the saving grace of humour, a humour which laughs through all cant and sham to the basic truths so far as man has yet been able to reach them.

IV. THE ARTIST

Mr. Robert Frost's poetry is a more complete revelation of his thoughts, observations, and emotions than any prose autobiography could ever be. It is not only a picture of him and of those close to him, but it is also a picture of that strange people north of Boston—those typical Yankees—among whom he grew up. He reveals not only their joys and ambitions, but their sorrows, disappointments, fears, and frustrations which often lead to madness. He appreciates and shares the canny common sense and shrewdness necessary to those who must extract a living from a rocky, hilly country. He not only knows the people as few know them—he sees in them the universal as well as the individual. His men and women are, as he says, 'types, composite and imagined people.' He understands and loves the country as few have done. He not only appreciates these things but he communicates with great subtlety his innermost feelings about them.

He neglects no season and finds in each an abundance of beauty. Nature speaks eloquently through him. Adequately to discuss his use of nature necessitates an examination of it as symbol, as metaphor, as texture, as mood, as atmosphere, as image. More truly, indeed, can we say of Mr. Frost than Amy Lowell said of herself that he *is* New England. But he is more than that; he is one of the few major poets America has yet given to the world. Because he wears his greatness with the true humility of genius, and because he is so truly the artist, the intellectual labour behind his poetry is apt to be missed. Mr. Frost has followed his own advice and has not hastened to bring his wares to market. Because he has done this there are fewer poems of his that a severe critic could wish away than of almost any other poet. It is only by chance that in the present chapter I shall be able to give a glimpse of the artist consciously at work.

Because of the manner in which Mr. Frost has clothed his

conclusions on life, he has at one time or other been called non-intellectual. This is, of course, to misunderstand him and his achievement. He is intellectual enough. As a poet, however, he is aware, as I have mentioned, of the value of colour. He is almost impressionistic in his concern for colour in his work. Because of his insistence on this quality—evident in his images, image-words, rhythms, and prosodic patterns, he achieves a correspondence with the reader otherwise impossible. The majority of his poems have an intellectual idea, but the idea is so transfused with emotion that it becomes knowledge and wisdom rather than cold fact. He knew, too, that wisdom came not so much from books as from an intelligent observation of life. He realized, too, as he grew older that although the colours of a poet's palette may become cooler, the emotion they evoke is no less profound. Petals are for youth; leaves for a darker mood as one grows older. As the winds of experience fan the leaves, he sees the stars. In his late years he emerges from the wood in order to have a fuller look at the skies. Because Mr. Frost's is a disciplined mind, he is able to grasp the emotion that lies above the purely intellectual, not only that which lies below it.

More has been written about Mr. Frost's blank verse than about any other of his prosodic achievements. This is understandable because his contribution is more readily apparent here than elsewhere. Actually, Mr. Frost has more than one blank verse style, although the difference is essentially a difference of degree. None of it is, strictly speaking, on the formal level. It varies from the colloquial, rather loosely textured verse of 'New Hampshire,' 'Build Soil,' and 'The Lesson for To-day,' to 'Out, Out—' and 'A Servant to Servants,' to 'Birches' and 'Mending Wall.' Blank verse is but one, however, of more than a hundred types of prosodic patterns which he has employed with varying degrees of success. Of these at least twenty-four are variations on the quatrain, seven on the cinquain, seven on the sixain, to mention but a few. Nor is blank verse the only type of unrhymed verse he has used. What we can say of Mr. Frost's blank verse can also be said of his couplets or poems with alternating rhymes.

What makes Mr. Frost's blank verse, his couplets, and other prosodic types original? The obvious answer is the highly conversational tone he achieves. The remarkable thing, however, is the regularity with which his blank verse scans. Occasionally he uses an eleven-syllable line, but not often. The basic pattern, too, is iambic. He achieves a contrapuntal effect by superimposing on this basic rhythm the less regular rhythm of speech. Illustration of this is not easy and will depend largely on the reader's ear. I feel, for example, a contrapuntal effect in the following:

> A better way to pass the afternoon
> Than grinding discord out of a grindstone,
> And beating insects at their gritty tune.
>
> 'The Grindstone'

Or in:

> Folks think a witch who has familiar spirits
> She could call up to pass a winter evening, . . .
>
> 'Two Witches'

I feel it everywhere in 'New Hampshire' and 'Build Soil.' He combines with this counterpoint a strongly colloquial diction varying from a high informal speech-level to one that is only slightly above the vulgate. He achieves this by the word order appropriate to that level and the use of dialect or colloquial words, as in the following use of 'wonted,' 'wa'n't,' 'drunk-nonsensical,' 'blame,' 'got so,' 'slim-jim,' and others:

> I must be *wonted* to it—that's the reason.
>
> 'Home Burial'

> If he *wa'n't* kept strict watch of,
>
> 'A Servant to Servants'

> I'm *drunk-nonsensical* tired out;
>
> 'In the Home Stretch'

> What do you want with one of those *blame* things?
> 'The Star-Splitter'

He heightens the tone by the occasional sentences of wisdom expressed in the homely idiom of the following:

> He says the best way out is always through
> 'A Servant to Servants'

> There's nothing I'm afraid of like scared people
> 'A Hundred Collars'

Every reader will think in this connection of some of Mr. Frost's deeply passionate definitions, like that of 'home' in 'The Death of the Hired Man,' and others.

More subtle, however, is his use of other figures in situations one would not expect from the general tone; yet they help to create that tone. Such is his use of alliteration on 's' and 'k' in 'Snow':

> Some of the sanctimonious conceit
> Out of one of those pious scalawags.

He combines alliteration with personification in the description of the white birch which stood alone,

> Wearing a thin head-dress of pointed leaves,
> And heavy on her heavy hair behind,
> Against her neck, an ornament of grapes, . . .
> 'Wild Grapes'

He often, too, uses repetition in his blank verse to heighten his effect. Repetition of 'sink,' for example, to heighten the sense of despair in 'In the Home Stretch':

> She stood against the kitchen sink, and looked
> Over the sink out through a dusty window
> At weeds the water from the sink made tall.

Or the repetition of 'one' in the opening of 'The Census Taker.'

Apart from these technical devices the form of the poems in blank verse are also responsible for their impact. Mr. Frost invariably begins his blank-verse poems disarmingly. Their casualness is more apparent than real. They give the sense of a person warming up for a talk-fest. The introduction is always, however, carefully proportioned to the poem's length, varying from two or three lines to the thirty-three of 'New Hampshire.' However long it is, it is never trivial nor unimportant. This general structural plan often leads the new reader astray into thinking that the first reading of the poem is enough. Mr. Frost never reveals himself to the casual reader any more than Schubert reveals himself to the casual listener.

What is true of Mr. Frost's blank verse is likewise true of his other poetry in differing degrees. He makes effective use of alliteration on 'f,' for example, in 'Stars,' 'The Impulse' from 'The Hill Wife,' and 'Desert Places.' He heightens his communication by repetition of 'without' in 'Going for Water,' of 'light' in 'The Trial by Existence,' of 'one' in 'Not of School Age,' and 'one' and 'release' in 'October,' and especially of 'lonely' and 'loneliness' with the accompanying alliteration on 'l' in 'Desert Places':

> The loneliness includes me unawares.
> And lonely as it is that loneliness
> Will be more lonely ere it will be less—

Mr. Frost's imagery never gives the impression of being tacked on or borrowed. It springs from his own observations of the world about him and, more frequently than a reader might suspect, from the world of literature, particularly from Shakespeare and some of the Latin poets. Nowhere is the poet's whole-hearted absorption in nature more clearly revealed than in his dependence on nature for vivifying an impression from the world of people. Pan's eyes were 'the gray of the moss of walls' ('Pan With Us'); the houses were sprinkled about the foot of the mountain 'like boulders broken off the upper cliff, Rolled out a little further than the rest' ('The Mountain'); the man had been choking 'like a nursery tree When it outgrows the wire band of its name tag' ('A Hundred Collars'); the poet's sorrow 'is glad her simple worsted gray Is silver now with clinging mist' ('My November Guest'); the star runs off in tangents 'as fish do with the line in first alarm' ('A Star in a Stone-Boat'). More fanciful is the flight of the butterfly tossed, tangled, and whirled 'like a limp rose-wreath in a fairy dance' ('My Butterfly'); but none is more revealing than the flame 'as slender as hepaticas Blood-root, and violets so soon to be now' ('The Bonfire').

The poet's powers of minute observation are not circumscribed. Little eludes him. The man's hand lies on his knee 'like a crumpled spider' ('Snow'); the benefits from a change of residence 'wore out like a prescription' ('A Servant to Servants'); the little boy is 'as pale and dim as a match flame in the sun' ('The Generations of Men'); the engine 'came breasting like a horse in skirts' ('The Egg and the Machine'); and Mrs. Baptiste's rocking-chair 'had as many motions as the world' ('The Axe-Helve').

Nowhere does Mr. Frost's real power more reveal itself, however, than in the single epithets he selects to illumine his subject. These range from the 'considerate neglect' of the widow ('The Black Cottage') to the clapboards of her cottage painted 'velvet black' by the shower. The lark is the 'daft sun-assaulter,' the humming-bird is the 'darting bird' and a 'meteor,' the chickadee has 'flirting' wings.[1] He notices that the stems of wild raspberries are purple ('Ghost House'), and he sees the fallen leaves as 'leathern' ('Maple'). The 'tumultuous snow' flows in 'shapes as tall as trees' ('Stars'), and the bonfire begins in a smudge with 'ropy' smoke ('The Bonfire'). He speaks, moreover, of the 'cramping' rafter ('The Vanishing Red'), the 'steel-bright' June grass ('The Exposed Nest'), the 'baritone' importance of the lawyer ('The Self-seeker'). The

---

[1] 'My Butterfly,' 'A Prayer in Spring,' 'Snow.'

red sky after sunset is 'the antiphony of afterglow' ('Waiting'),
the telegraph-pole is 'a resurrected tree' ('An Encounter'),
the lantern-light from deep in the barn throws the 'lurking
shadows' of the man and woman on a house where all was
dark in every 'glossy window' ('The Fear'). The croaking of
the frogs in the fen that 'rang all night' ('In a Vale'), and the
voice that 'came scraping slow' ('Snow') are only further
examples from a great abundance.

It is not only the evocative or pictorial quality of the words
that is characteristic of Mr. Frost; it is also their selection for
their sound. He can so choose and arrange common words
that they perform an affective as well as an informative
function. Perhaps this is more evident in passages rather than
single words that reveal his powers of observation. His
descriptions of blueberries, for example, implies not only a
visual but a tactile experience:

> And after all really, they're ebony skinned:
> The blue's but a mist from the breath of the wind,
> A tarnish that goes at the touch of the hand.
>
> 'Blueberries'

'Tarnish' is only one of many excellencies in the description.
He goes beyond the present to the future, and thereby en-
riches the immediate:

> The leaves are all dead on the ground,
> Save those that the oak is keeping
> To *ravel* them one by one
> And let them go *scraping* and *creeping*
> Out over the crusted snow,
> When others are sleeping.
>
> 'Reluctance'

Cause and effect unite in the orchard tree that

> . . . has grown one *copse*
> Of new wood and old where the woodpecker chops:
>
> 'Ghost House'

A sense of humour intrudes when 'he struck the clapboards' and 'fierce heads looked out; small bodies pivoted' ('The Black Cottage').

Mr. Frost uses personification sparingly, but when he does, he is fresh and vigorous. Two examples will suffice. The first is a vivid evocation of wind:

> The three stood listening to a fresh access
> of wind that caught against the house a moment,
> *Gulped snow*, and then blew free again. . . .
>
> 'Snow'

The second suggests the living quality of decay:

> The warping boards pull out their own old nails
> With none to tread and put them in their place.
>
> 'The Black Cottage'

Each careful reader will find for himself those that will increase his opinion of Mr. Frost's artistry.

Early drafts of Mr. Frost's published poems are not readily available. By a happy chance I can throw a little light on the way he builds a poem. On the fly-leaf of the first American edition of *A Boy's Will* in my possession is an early draft of 'Nature's first green is gold,' inscribed by Mr. Frost, dated May, 1922. Here is the draft:

> Nature's first green is gold,
> Her hardest hue to hold.
> Her early leaves are flowers
> But only so for hours;
> Then leaves subside to leaves.
> In autumn she achieves
> A still more golden blaze,
> But nothing golden stays.

Although good, it is inferior to the published version. Whether the later addition of the image of Eden was directly responsible for the change of 'leaves' and 'flowers' to the singular is impossible to say. In any case, the change was inevitable. The 'z' sound of the plural lacks finality. It suspends the sense rather than clinches it, especially in conjunction with the number of liquids of the early lines. The alteration, too, of the 'v' of leaves to the 'f' of 'leaf' is more direct. Notice the improvement:

> Nature's first green is gold,
> Her hardest hue to hold.
> Her early leaf's a flower;
> But only so an hour.
> Then leaf subsides to leaf.

The next two lines of the draft are pure nature-observation. They are of the first level of meaning with no universal import. The insertion of the beautiful analogy of Eden changes the meaning. It not only gives a broader significance but flushes a long train of associative memories. Even the most perfect of God's favoured spots could not escape decay, although in the case of Eden it was through the fault of man and the loss of innocence:

> So Eden sank to grief.

The next change continues the thought.

> So dawn goes down to day.

This line carries several meanings, the third level of meaning is that the rosy confidence of innocence gives way to the stronger light of experience. This does not mean that idealism gives way to disillusionment; but it does suggest that idealism must be based on an understanding of the ways of the world.

The final line of the draft—But nothing golden stays—is loose-textured. Mr. Frost gives it much greater force in the published version by the change to 'Nothing gold can stay.' 'Can' is forceful and final. Man must realize that all beauty, all glory, is but transient. Changes made in the poem are characteristic of the inner change in Mr. Frost. His early sensuousness becomes more tightly controlled by his reason.

Mr. Frost reveals his great artistry, too, in the care with which he has fitted his prosodic pattern to his thought to create the desired effect. So expertly does he achieve this that the careless reader is apt to think that it just happened. It is possible to conceive that a poem may occasionally write itself, particularly if it is a short lyric, but such occasions are rare. Mr. Frost is not one to trust to chance. In 'A Leaf Treader,' for example, he sought to communicate the fatigue resulting from a healthy day of autumn tramping. He achieves this by the use of a seven-stress line, strongly anapestic in character. He has been led into the acceptance of a state that is not a customary one. The fall of the leaves, determined to carry him to death, almost brought him to surrender.

They spoke to the fugitive in my heart as if it were leaf
    to leaf
They tapped at my eyelids and touched my lips with an
    invitation to grief.

At this moment, however, he recovers control over himself; his courage to live reasserts itself. The rhythms catch and emphasize this change:

But it was no reason I had to go because they had to go.
Now up my knee to keep on top of another year of snow.

He gives a strongly satiric flavour to 'An Imposter' by his use of couplets in trochaic tetrameter and a factual one to 'On Making Certain Anything Has Happened' by a stanza in couplets of iambic trimeter. I cannot recall an instance where after a second or third reading the outward form seemed unsuitable to the occasion. This is as true of the poems in *A Witness Tree* and *Steeple Bush* as of those in the earlier volumes.

*   *   *   *   *

To compare Mr. Frost with Hardy may seem a supererogation. On the surface, as I have suggested, no two poets are more unlike. Yet *The Masque of Reason* and *The Masque of*

Mercy contain ideas not so different from some of Hardy's ideas as one might suppose. The ideas are seen, however, from different points of view. Frost looks at them from that of a man who never for a moment compromised with his most deeply-based beliefs and convictions as a thinker and as an artist. He has lived to see the complete justification of his stand. He can see, therefore, all that Hardy sees, but he can look at it with a spirit of affirmation. Hardy sees ideas from the point of view of one who compromised with himself as an artist at a critical time in his development. Not only, therefore, did he never achieve the same degree of artistry as Mr. Frost, but his defection from what he knew within himself to be the correct thing for him distorted his perspective of reality.

We have already examined the idea on which Frost has built his poems. He does not write of the subject as an observer, but as one who has experienced its innermost mysteries and is richer for the experience. He is aware, too, that the style of age must differ from the style of youth if one has grown. He has demonstrated in *Steeple Bush* that in a lyric he can achieve the necessary tightness of texture. The same tightness or density, to change the metaphor, is out of place in works like *The Masque of Reason* and *The Masque of Mercy* where he has aimed at communicating the tolerance and wisdom of age. In none of his longer poems are there so many memorable passages, so much food for thought, so much ripeness of observation. Because he has not flinched from facing reality and has adjusted himself to it, he is more free from pessimism than any other modern poet. Of all the poets in the present selection he is the one who has seen most clearly. By never 'straddling' he has kept the clarity of his vision unimpaired. By ridding himself of fear he has been able gracefully to accept what has overwhelmed many. He has maintained a refreshing sanity.

G

WALLACE STEVENS
(1879—   )

Part I

MR. WALLACE STEVENS has the anomalous position of being one of America's most important poets, but also one of her least known. None gives the impression of more careful craftsmanship, or a greater jewel-like precision. From his early poems never included in a volume, however, it would have been impossible to foresee the direction his later development would take. Between 1901, when his work was strictly conventional in the nineteenth-century popular idiom, and 1915, he had so changed his style that he was one of the 'others' in the *avant garde* group that included T. S. Eliot, Alfred Kreymbourg, Marianne Moore, Ezra Pound, Carl Sandburg, and others. Unfortunately, although understandably, the work most frequently available in anthologies is from his first volume *Harmonium*. Unfortunately, because although charming, humorous, and provocative, like 'Peter Quince at the Clavier,' these poems fail to convey adequately Mr. Stevens' stature. 'Le Monocle de Mon Oncle,' 'Invective Against Swans,' and 'The Comedian as the Letter C' do, however, foreshadow the solidity of his later work. Understandably, however, because the poems in this earlier volume are more easily grasped.

Mr. Stevens is a difficult poet; one of the most difficult I have ever read. But the effort expended pays adequate dividends. He is an aristocrat in the fullest and best sense of the term. He is no ivory-towerist, accepts his mundane responsibilities (he holds an important executive position in a large insurance company), yet remains aloof. He feels no

necessity to fraternize with the men in the street because he
must perforce move among them. He is aware of the
materialism about him, but also adheres to his ideals. He is
not a cold cosmopolite, only a reserved and shy one; fastidious,
not precious.

It is true, I think, that many of the themes of the poems in
Harmonium lack significance. Like 'Peter Quince at the
Clavier,' they are virtuoso pieces, or at best musical moments.
But Mr. Stevens has something to say worth listening to.
The serious reader will not, however, find his problem
simple. Once he makes out what he thinks is the central idea
of the poem, he will fail of a strong aesthetic response because
the parts will not seem to him to be carefully integrated.
He senses the disjointedness that many feel to be a characteristic of modern society. Form is not lacking, but it is not
apparent. One reason is Mr. Stevens' symbolism which, to
all appearances, is pretty much a private affair; another is his
diction, particularly his vocabulary. Words carry an esoteric
meaning. Let us attempt, however, a synthesis of Mr. Stevens'
ideas.

Mr. Stevens' aim is the same as that of Shelley: to appeal to
the spiritual-intellectual and to hope that through him his
ideas will percolate to the broader strata below. His poetry
aims at the noble, and its object is, by making man aware of
himself, to lead him to a higher spiritual life. His finest
expression of these aims is his poetry. He recognizes that his
poetry must be living, must use the speech of his time, must
address the men and women of to-day, and must find what will
suffice for man in modern society. The poet, opposing life
as it is, would change it to something more significant.
Although he draws his strength from his worldly contacts, he
struggles to find the impossible ideal in Utopias of the mind.
Impossible because he seeks it in surroundings in a constant
state of flux. The poet's function is for Mr. Stevens more

than the spinning of beautiful-sounding phrases. He seeks the greater reality and would 'reconcile us to ourselves.'[1]

He suggests that in the springtime of life, when he was less despondent over things as they are than he later became, he thought the aesthetic life adequate. He found, however, that such a life could not bring happiness. Even were he able to lose himself—'the evilly compounded, vital I'—and make 'it fresh in a world of white' he would still want more. No 'never-resting mind' could be content in an ideal existence, a symbol of which is a perpetual vacation in Florida. Better is the winter slime of the north 'both of men and clouds, a slime of men in crowds,' where he partakes of their 'violent minds.' Delight lies 'in flawed words and stubborn sounds.'[2]

What, we may profitably ask, is the nature of this world in which the poet finds himself? Mr. Stevens makes a sharp distinction between the man of the open spaces and indus-trialized man. Even though ours be a tragic time with little beauty in modern garishness, life in the open is healthy, courageous, active, and free; in the city not. Men are little more than 'mechanical beetles never quite warm,' or mice who go around in a meaningless routine of activities from which little nobility is possible.[3]

His objection to the masses is that

> The men have no shadows
> And the women have only one side.
>
> 'The Common Life'

He feels that the swift (sensitive) are undiscriminated from the slow, and that the gods of modern life are of little worth. Only the ignorant and the vulgar can think life satisfactory. Despite an outward manner of specious importance, the

[1] 'Of Modern Poetry,' 'Mozart, 1935,' 'A Fish-Scale Sunrise,' 'The Man with the Blue Guitar,' 'Poetry Is a Destructive Force,' 'Academic Discourse at Havana,' 'The Man on the Dump.'

[2] 'The Sun this March,' 'The Poems of Our Climate,' 'A Farewell to Florida.'

[3] 'Parochial Theme,' 'Yellow Afternoon,' 'Dry Loaf,' 'Anything Is Beautiful If You Say It Is,' 'Dance of Macabre Mice,' 'The Man with the Blue Guitar.'

essence of modern man is an inner worthlessness. The times
are not conducive to spiritual richness. Although incessant
strife exists between employer and employee, some indications
point to a spiritual awakening; but, certainly, it would be a
great mistake to think an isolated instance the herald of a
general mass movement. Subtle definitions cannot conceal the
awful truth that men as a whole are pretty poor specimens
and are little likely to be different. The lives of these mass-
men are not lived; their days are wasted. They have been
'baffled by the trash of life.'[1]

Mr. Stevens recognizes the obvious; that the worker could
not possibly achieve culture at one jump. It must evolve
slowly. But his criticism is that the worker has none of that
pioneer spirit that earlier braved the west. These pioneers
found the meaning of life in themselves—in just being. The
industrial workers desire this same joy, but, trying to reach it
by a different route, achieve spiritual death instead. They sense
that a change is necessary, that they are seeking an un-
apprehended goal, but they are confused. Herded and told
what to think, they cannot articulate for themselves their
desires, nor will they ever have that ability. Gloomy as this
picture is, but unfortunately largely true, the poet recognizes
that the most potent force is sometimes necessity, and suggests
that

> These voices crying without knowing for what,
> Except to be happy, without knowing how,
> Imposing forms they cannot describe,
> Requiring order beyond their reach—

may sometime be united and their desires crystallized. On the
whole he finds little order in the world except as the artist is

---

[1] 'Loneliness in Jersey City,' 'The Bagatelles the Madrigals,' 'The Man with the
Blue Guitar, xxx-xxxiii.'

able to create it through his imagination, in which, however, one cannot always dwell. The times are out of joint and instead of peace and tranquillity, fear and hate are rife and war impends.[1]

Mr. Stevens does not believe that his poetry can markedly alter the world. It presents a reality not readily apparent to the average, and those capable of reading his poetry are not the average. They are aware of the same reality as he. Its value, then, is the intensification of their convictions about reality. Because of it he may be able to patch the world, even though he cannot remake it.

He rejects the sentimental idea that nature is the kind mother of us all and recognizes that she is a cruel oppressor who begrudges us living our lives. He finds, too, a definite value in the complete contact with reality. Only, in fact, by this stark knowledge can he attain his own spiritual self that can resist the disintegrating forces of life. Only thus can he prevent himself becoming one monster in the midst of many; only thus can he *be*, or in part attain to, that intelligence which can interpret the world to itself. Reason is not enough; faith and a vision capable of seeing that the future contains 'pasts destroyed' are both necessary.[2]

Powerful force though the mind is, capable of looking through the superficial and finding what will suffice in a time of war and trouble, it cannot find the absolutes. Heaven lies about the seeing man in his sensuous apprehension of the world (and Mr. Stevens masterfully evokes that world for the sensitive reader); everything about him is part of the truth. The factory worker seeks heaven in Communism, but without success. Heaven (or happiness), however, is often the com-

---

[1] 'Owl's Clover,' 'Sad Strains for a Gay Waltz,' 'United Dames of America,' 'Mud Master,' 'Woman Looking at a Vase of Flowers,' 'Add This to Rhetoric,' 'Girl in a Nightgown.'

[2] 'The Man with the Blue Guitar,' 'Owl's Clover.'

plete abandonment of oneself to a life of sensation and feeling.[1]
It may be, suggests the poet,

> . . . that the ignorant man, alone,
> Has any chance to mate life with life
> That is sensual, pearly spouse, the life
> That is fluent in even the wintriest bronze.

This latter idea, however, is not an unaltering conviction.
Such thoughts painfully hammered out at night are moods
common to all who seek order in our world; they vanish in
the activities of the day. The person most tortured by these
thoughts on man and the condition of modern society eagerly
longs for the day. Although those following us seem to have
been spirits 'storming in blank walls,' we were at one time as
alive and eager in the pursuit of life as they, and have left our
imprint.[2]

In spite of his awareness of many monuments of a richer
past, the poet feels the present to be barren and unproductive.
The rich, particularly, so cherish these mementoes of a dying
past that they are unable to lose themselves in and partake
richly of the present. They fail to realize that 'what's above is
in the past As sure as all the angels are,' although he concurs
with them in their belief that there is so little on earth over
which to rejoice that man needs the idea of a hereafter or the
sop of religion to give meaning to life.[3] The average man, on
the other hand, is poorer for his obliviousness to the meaning
of men of the past who achieved so much and were of such a
different stature. It is natural for a sensitive person to feel
that in a congenial atmosphere of spirituality his own development would have been greater. He realizes that too much of
his effort must be spent in resisting Philistinism. He is

[1] 'Man and Bottle,' 'The Search for Sound Free from Motion,' 'The Blue Buildings,'
'In the Summer Air,' 'Landscape with Boat,' 'Of Bright Blue Birds and the Gala Sun,'
'The Sense of the Sleight-of-Hand Man.'
[2] 'The Brave Man,' 'On the Adequacy of Landscape,' 'A Postcard from the Volcano.'
[3] 'Cuisine Bourgeoise,' 'Arcades of Philadelphia the Past,' 'Botanist on Alp (No. 2).'

gradually forced to the conviction that our daily activities lead us nowhere. Man assumes importance *in* the world by giving importance *to* the world. He needs this in order to save himself from despair. Some, however, aware of the folly of running in circles and cognizant of the fact that what we take from life comes from ourselves and is our only reward, insist upon striving toward a greater consciousness of life. This is tantamount to a constant leave-taking from those content with their lot. Conditioned as we become through reason to living in an unspiritual world, we are still capable of moments of ecstasy from bird-song or other natural phenomena of the land, sky, and sea. Unfortunately, however, the sensuous delight of the early years when 'to be and delight to be seemed one' cannot last. At such a passing one begins to dwell in the past.[1]

What, actually, is the meaning of life? is a question the poet continually poses to himself. Is there any? Is it only chance that we are what we are? Although he once sought faith, justice, patience, and fortitude (which he never found), he later realized that his great desire was to make unseeing man the sharer in his love for the sensuous beauty of the natural world, to make him aware of a noble ideal of self, to give him a vision of the heroic which would stimulate him to a greater spiritual activity, to awaken him to the fact that it is what one *is* that is important.[2]

Mr. Stevens is by no means a pessimist. He is an idealist who maintains his idealism in the midst of a realistic world and with a full consciousness of that world. Rage though he may against the chaos of the world, he nevertheless has a sense of the islands of goodness open to whoever seeks. He experienced this feeling, without understanding it, as he walked to church. After every negation, too, he felt the

---

[1] 'Dance of the Macabre Mice,' 'The Latest Freed Man,' 'Waving Adieu, Adieu, Adieu,' 'Meditation Celestial and Terrestrial,' 'Anglais Mort à Florence.'

[2] 'Lions in Sweden,' 'The Men that are Falling,' 'Country Words,' 'The Pleasures of Merely Circulating.'

necessity for affirmation—and experienced it, particularly when he was free from the fettering environment of the average man. With man's restless mind, however, how is he to arrive at a final belief? Perhaps man is not enough, but beyond this is 'the impossible possible philosopher's man' who has time to get to the 'central man, the human glove.' He alone is able in the midst of war to synthetize it with the sum of his other experiences. Few things exist for or are sufficient unto themselves. Everywhere one sees a violent order in disorder (Germany, for example) and a great disorder in an order (perhaps the U.S.A.), but he also recognizes the chaotic disorder of life's many truths, and a continuing disorder. Inequalities will thrive, the poor will be always with us, and no -ism will be able to resolve the difficulties.[1] Man's fate, therefore, lies within himself. He who seizes and attempts to subdue us merely wants to be at the centre of all the parts and control all the spread. He wants, in other words, to play the rôle of God, to find himself supremely.

To experience the sublime in a world of false values and 'plated pairs,' each must be true to himself in spite of his surroundings. Clear vision of the way may be obstructed by the masses, but the time is more than ripe for the coming of love to 'this mangled, smutted semi-world hacked out of dirt.'[2] What, he asks, remains for him to love that he has not loved? If there are other greater things, he would willingly say amen to those he has enjoyed. His deeper humanity desires to instil in the mind of unthinking man those spiritual qualities of the hero by which he can find in himself through the vivifying powers of the imagination 'the grace And free requiting of responsive fact.' In other words, he wishes man to awaken to the truth that the riches of the world are nothing

---

[1] 'Winter Bells,' 'Evening Without Angels,' 'The Well-Dressed with a Beard,' 'Asides on the Oboe,' 'Les Plus Belles Pages,' 'Idiom of the Hero,' 'Life on a Battleship.'
[2] 'The American Sublime,' 'How to Live. What to Do,' 'Ghosts as Cocoons.'

more than the projection of himself on the phenomena of that world.[1]

One of Mr. Stevens' longest poems, 'Extracts from Addresses to the Academy of Fine Ideas,' crystallizes the foregoing ideas. Civilization, he believes, is artificial compared to the real things, such as the seas, sky, and nature in general. To separate the real from the false, however, is difficult because the eye is easily deceived by appearances, and too often some escape life by a complete withdrawal from the world into their ivory towers. In this lies death. It is necessary to face the world of fact before it is possible to attain a higher one. America, for example, although she possesses great optimism, courage, and faith in the future, lacks the sense of design that the leaner European possesses. No single aim unites the people, and in the multitude of thoughts by which men constantly struggle to find the right answer to life, they meet death rather than life. Chaos rather than order is the result until one person dominates the rest. His solution is no more valid than others. Actually, says the poet, there is no one right idea. The person seeking the ultimate order must not look for it, therefore, in the mass-mind, but in his own mind. The world has meaning only as the mind gives meaning to it. Only what the mind believes is what matters, and our only salvation lies in our own hearts, not in any idea of an after-life.

The poet is useful in society because knowledge of anything is only possible through metaphor—through feeling. In other words, true affirmation is that of the imagination and only in the imagination can one free oneself from the negations of reality. It is more powerful, in fact, than reality and gives a stature to things they would not otherwise possess. Not only is it a freeing agent from the petty annoyances of the day, but it permits us to invest fact with an idea, to apprehend

[1] 'Montrachet-le-Jardin,' 'Phosphor Reading by His Own Light.'
[2] 'Poem Written at Morning,' 'Delightful Evening.'

the world that lies about us. Mr. Stevens has said that his desire is to equate the 'root-man with the super-man,' to implant the heroic ideal in the average mind.

It is important to understand his concept of the hero, one of the most persistent themes in his poetry. The most comprehensive exposition of this idea occurs in 'Examination of the Hero in Time of War.' No statue can do the hero justice—it is the pinching or constricting of an idea. Parades in his honour are profane vulgarizations of the real idea. No person is the hero. There is no image of the hero. He is an idealization and extension of the finest qualities of a man magnified in all directions and not verifiable by fact, not even by the actions of a soldier in battle. He is a feeling—'a man seen As if the eye was an emotion'—who can only be appreciated if we ourselves possess the 'brave quickenings' of his nature. 'To meditate the highest man,' says the poet, 'creates, in the blissfuller perceptions, What unisons create in music,' an apprehension of the sublime.

This leads, of course, to the truism that we get from life only what we take to it. Every response depends upon our conditioning, and what is true for one is false for another. It is difficult to find this happiness in oneself when all about are crying for help; yet the only real joy that one can know and be certain of lies within oneself. That alone makes the world sweet. The poet alone denies that abstraction is a vice, because in the midst of concrete manifestations of man he finds happiness in the abstract idea of man and the changing concept of God. He alone comprehends the hero. He alone seeks for the man possessed of godlike attributes who possesses his heaven within himself and who yet remains a man.[1]

Convinced that imagination is the greatest force for life in this world, it is only natural that one of his latest poems, 'Esthètique du Mal,' should concern itself wholly with the

---

[1] 'Mrs. Alfred Uruguay,' 'Poems with Rhythms,' 'A Rabbit as King of the Ghosts,' 'Sailing after Lunch,' 'Examination of the Hero in Time of War,' 'On the Road Home,' 'A Fading of the Sun,' 'The Idea of Order at Key West,' 'A Thought Revolved.'

power of imagination. The ideas differ little from those found scattered among his poems, except perhaps for his attitude toward pain as a beneficent force that heightens one's awareness to the world. 'Satan's death,' says Mr. Stevens, 'was a tragedy for the imagination.' It is interesting that many of the ideas of the relatively early 'The Comedian as the Letter C' parallel those of 'Esthètique du Mal.' As sheer poetry, however, the later poem possesses far greater richness than the earlier.

It would be unfair to leave the discussion of Mr. Stevens' ideas without some mention of his attitude toward nature. Resentful as he may be toward the deadening life of the city and the automata from the various strata of society that maintain a constant movement in concentric circles, he is at his most gracious in the presence of the ever-changing phenomena of nature. And I think he is resentful merely because he would like others to share in his sensuous apprehension of the universe. In these poems the reader will find ample evidence for the richness and scope of the poet's powerful imagination and nobility of soul. Here, too, he will find the poet freed from the fret of thinking and his spirit full-blown. Yet one should remember that the values and importance he attaches to these un-human affections stem from a full look at the worst.[1]

Shorn of the vivifying powers of his imagination and oversimplified as is the foregoing statement of his ideas, it is clear that his basic ideas have significance. How much greater must be the full statement!

[1] 'Dezembrum,' 'Of Hartford in a Purple Light,' 'Contrary Theses (1),' 'Contrary Theses (2),' 'The Candle. A Saint,' 'Some Friends from Pascagoula,' 'The News and the Weather,' 'Metamorphosis,' 'Martial Cadenza,' 'Study of Two Pears,' 'The Glass of Water,' 'Gray Stones and Gray Pigeons,' 'Snow and Stars,' 'Autumn Refrain,' 'The Reader,' 'Botanist on Alp (No. 1),' 'A Dish of Peaches in Russia,' 'Like Decorations in a Nigger Cemetery,' 'Re-Statement of Romance,' 'Gallant Chateau,' 'The Hand as Being.'

PART II

The reason that Mr. Stevens is a little-known poet lies not, then, in the validity of his materials but in the demand he makes upon the reader for grasping those ideas. His conviction is that the poet 'fulfils himself only as he sees his imagination become the light in the mind of others'; his difficulty is that only in the minds of a select few of the serious readers of poetry does his imagination become the light he desires it to be. A knowledge of some of the technical difficulties may help the uninitiated to penetrate the clouds.

To the poet only the exact meaning can suffice, because only by his precision of meaning can he control the emotions of his reader. As Mr. Stevens has developed as a poet, he has been increasingly conscious of this need. The difference is obvious between what now strikes us as the loose and effusive diction of the poems of his youth and the carefully chosen, highly compressed quality of his later work. Since his passion is truth, he has sought avidly for the word which will correctly communicate his subtlest nuance. 'The deepening need for words to express one's thought and feelings,' he has written, 'which, we are sure, are all the truth that we shall ever experience, having no illusions, makes us listen to words when we hear them, loving them and feeling them, makes us search the sound of them, for a finality, a perfection, and unalterable vibration, which it is only within the power of the acutest poet to give them.' He does not confine himself to an accurate use of the familiar word as does Mr. Frost; he employs such less familiar ones as 'malison,' 'maladive,' 'perjorative,' 'bezeled,' and 'panache.' He coins words to suit his purpose, such as 'skreak' and 'skritter,' 'spissantly' (to rhyme with 'puissantly'), and others. He uses, too, familiar words in startling combinations. This is legitimate, of course, if he is content with a limited audience. It is the esoteric modern poet, however, who often turns a potential reader from poetry.

Mr. Stevens resembles Hopkins in his care in the manipulation of vowels and consonants. In the following couplet:

> His slowly-falling round
> Down to the fishy sea—
> > 'Some Friends from Pascagoula'

the vowels move from front to back then return to front. The poet follows no set formula, and he is capable of inweaving his melodies at almost every emotional level from grave to gay, from simple statement to caustic acerbity. He loves alliteration, sometimes so much that it masters him. Here we find some of his more esoteric words. The vibration which he receives from the combination fails to set up a similar one in his most sympathetic reader. Interesting as are some of the following examples from the point of view of sound, do they heighten the communication of the basic idea? They have a youthful appeal, perhaps, but little more. They are too self-consciously clever:

> He carolled in caracoles
> On the feat sandbars.
> > 'The Jack Rabbit'

> Chieftan Iffucan of Azcan in caftan
> Of tan with henna hackles, halt!
> > 'Bantams in Pine Woods'

> Call the roller of big cagars,[1]
> The muscular one, and bid him whip
> In kitchen cups concupiscent curds.
> > 'The Emperor of Ice-Cream'

What, in the name of heaven, are 'concupiscent curds'? These are all from *Harmonium* (1923). The unrestrained tendency is

[1] See note on p. 101.

brought under greater control in his intermediate work and
disappears almost entirely in his latest:

> . . . against the prester,[1]
> Presto, whose whispers prickle the spirit.
>> 'Examination of the Hero in Time of War'
> . . . the psalter of their sybils.
>> *Ibid.*
> The chick, the chidder-barn[1] and grassy chives.
>> 'Montrachet-le-Jardin'
> In the first canto of the final canticle.
>> 'The Hand as Being'
> The prince of proverbs of pure poetry.
>> 'Esthètique du Mal'

Often, too, the selection of place-names is determined by
alliteration rather than by geographical necessity. The only
valid reason for selecting Bogota instead of some other South
American city is that it alliterates with 'beggar'—'beggar of
Bogota'; or for Pomerania, than that it is amusing in combination with 'poodles'—'poodles of Pomerania.' The same is
true of 'cock-robins' at 'Caracas'. Generally speaking, however, the alliterating compounds, such as 'flame-freaked sun,'
'plated pairs,' 'micky mockers,' and others heighten the poetic
impact.

Mr. Stevens uses no trite image-words. Occasionally we
have the unusual 'lacustrine man,' but more often we find them
provocative as the 'clickering syllables,' 'one chemical afternoon,' life as 'a bitter aspic,' Vesuvius is 'pain audible at
noon,' 'the sun-costuming clouds,' 'the dove with eyes of
grenadine.' He is unbelievably accurate in 'the blessed regal
[lily] dropped in dagger's dew,' and 'the many stanzaed sea.'
At times, too, he achieves his image by coining variations of
the conventional, generally for comic or satiric effect, and
with an internal rhyme. Instance, for example, 'all afternoon
the gramaphoon,' or for October—'oto-otu-bre.' This ono-

---

[1] 'Cagars,' and 'chidder-barn' seem to be coinages of the poet; 'prester' is 'priest.'

matopoeic tendency finds greatest crystallization in such poems as 'Mozart, 1935,' or parts of 'The Man with the Blue Guitar.' The present disorganized jazz spirit is sharply envisaged in the following:

> Poet, be seated at the piano,
> Play the present, its hoo-hoo-hoo,
> Its shoo-shoo-shoo, its ric-a-rac,
> Its envious cachination.

And:

> To strike his living hi and ho
> To tick it, tock it, turn it true.

Where Mr. Stevens reveals himself a first-rate poet, however, is in his sustained images. He has said repeatedly that we can have a knowledge of something only by metaphor. His own practice furnishes abundant testimony that he is capable of communicating to the reader the accuracy of his perceptions. His range is wide. He can be fastidiously elegant, sensitive beyond most to the natural and elemental world about him, humorously tolerant, witty, grimly humorous, and deeply moved by the horror frequently presented by the spectacle of the vulgarity and depravity of mankind.

I can only suggest the riches that the attentive reader will find wherever he turns in his poetry, a richness greater than one at first deems possible. Whether it is the unusual description of what the night is not and what the night is in 'Dezembrum,' the tone of satiety with the endless image-making of poets in the satiric 'The Man on the Dump,' the strong but horrible image of 'A Weak Mind in the Mountains,' he brings to his images a quality of independence and full awareness of the world about him. Different from the usual picture of a river is that in 'Frogs Eat Butterflies, etc.,' with its comparison to swine:

> It is true that the river went nosing like swine,
> Tugging at banks, until they seemed
> Bland belly-sounds in somnolent troughs.

In the later afternoon of 'Gray Stones and Gray Pigeons,'

> A dithery gold falls everywhere,
> It wets the pigeons,
> It goes and the birds go,
> Turn dry, . . .

Or, the dogwoods were

> . . . the sheets high up on older trees
> Seeming to be liquid as leaves made of cloud,
> Shells under water
> > 'Forces, the Will and the Weather'

Often an entire poem becomes a sustained image or a symbol. It is the poet's symbolism that constitutes the greatest barrier to understanding. One frequently longs for a gloss to make easier the grasp of a poem as a whole. A second reading frequently, however, makes clear symbols that were at first elusive. The reader familiar with Picasso's powerful depiction from his blue period of an old blind man playing the guitar will perhaps be better prepared to understand 'The Man with the Blue Guitar' than one who approaches the poem without that associative aid. The communication of many parts of the poem even after several readings remains blurred. 'Owl's Clover,' 'Life on a Battleship,' and the early 'The Comedian as the Letter C' are sustained examples of a characteristic often encountered in single stanzas of shorter poems. The inability fully to grasp the symbol makes impossible a complete aesthetic reaction to the poem and prevents Mr. Stevens' imagination becoming 'the light in the minds of others.' Such symbols as the sunlight representing reality, moonlight and summer the functioning of the imagination, winter as the light of reason, and the statue as the symbol of the hero are understandable. So, too, is that of the rocky wastes as symbolic of the lack of spirituality of modern civilization, because of its familiarity in the work of Mr. Eliot. But many readers would welcome help from the poet in the

H

form of notes. More than any other thing, the failure to understand his symbolism keeps many readers from him who could share and sympathize with his attitude toward life. Time will remove many of the difficulties.

Mr. Stevens is supremely the poet in his verbal harmonies. His music is subtle. So masterful is he in controlling these harmonies that even without a complete grasp of the intellectual concept behind the poem, the reader shares the poet's emotional reaction to the fecundating idea. The music is unlike that of any other poet. A strong tradition is at the root of his harmonies, but he has altered the tradition. He can make the reader feel cramped or can impart a sense of largeness; can make him laugh or make him withdraw in horror; arouse pity or make him a sharer in the graciousness of life; take him with him into the most fastidious and elegant atmosphere, force him into too close a contact with crass vulgarity to be comfortable, or, as in 'Montrachet-le-Jardin,' inspire in him a large nobility of soul.

The rhythms of the early poems in *Harmonium* are far less subtle than those in *Parts of a World* and *Esthètique du Mal*. There is a charming lilt to 'Peter Quince at the Clavier' and 'Country Words,' but I prefer those of 'Le Monocle de Mon Oncle,' 'Connoisseur of Chaos,' 'Forces, the Will and the Weather,' and 'Esthètique du Mal.'

Mr. Stevens places little reliance in rhyme, although he is a master of it when he thinks it will serve his purpose. He makes greater use of repetition and turns. Quotation is difficult, because lifted from its context much of the charm of a passage disappears. 'Autumn Refrain,' however, may serve as an illustration:

The skreak and skritter of the evening gone
And grackles gone and sorrows of the sun,
The sorrows of the sun, too, gone . . . the moon and moon,
The yellow moon of words about the nightingale
In measureless measures, not a bird for me

But the name of a bird and the name of a nameless air
I have never—shall never hear. And yet beneath
The stillness of everything gone, and being still,
Being and sitting still, something resides,
Some skreaking and skrittering residuum,
And grates these evasions of the nightingale
Though I have never—shall never hear that bird.
And the stillness is in the key, all of it is,
The stillness is all in the key of that desolate sound.

Mr. Stevens' deftness in keying the desired emotional mood
to his rhythms is evident in 'The Idea of Order at Key West'
and often in 'Esthètique du Mal.' Many readers, however,
would be repelled rather than attracted by so conscious a
manipulation of sounds as in the following:

A vessel sinks in waves
Of people, as big bell-billows from its bell
Bell-billow in the village steeple. Violets,
Great tufts, spring up from buried houses
Of poor dishonest people for whom the steeple,
Long since, rang out, farewell, farewell, farewell.
                                        'Esthètique du Mal'

But few would deny the beauty of the passages from the same
poem beginning, 'How red the rose that is the soldier's wound'
and 'The peopled and unpeopled.' It is impossible to give in
an essay an adequate idea of the scope of Mr. Stevens' successful experiments in stanza forms. Whether he uses the rhymed
couplet, tercet, quatrain, or a longer form, he gives it the
impress of his own personality. He is never the careless nor
hurried craftsman. Only by continued association can one
sense the carefully controlled but deeply passionate quality of
his work. His stature as a poet is only slowly grasped. He
should be more largely known, more understandingly read
both by the small coterie of admirers and by the passionate
lovers of truth. Few have the time or the willingness to make

the effort to understand him. Poems like 'Of Modern Poetry' and 'The Dwarf' have a crystalline clarity; but such poems as 'Oak Leaves are Hands' remain but dimly apprehended emotion arising from a combination of sounds that create a humorous response. Personally, I feel an incompleteness of response. Between these extremes lie sections of 'The Man with the Blue Guitar,' parts of 'Owl's Clover,' and numerous short poems. One of his latest works, 'Esthètique du Mal,' is relatively clear at the first or second reading and is certainly one of his most beautiful poems. Only by the ability to grasp a poem with the mind as well as to feel it with the heart, can the reader avoid that sense of frustration which arises from an incomplete aesthetic experience. To grasp the whole necessitates a certainty of the parts; and verbal harmony is not enough for an unqualified sense of aesthetic completeness.

Quite obviously Mr. Stevens has ranged wide in his reading. He draws from the classics, popular songs like 'Harvest Moon,' ritual, the French symbolists, and the modern poets. He tends to assume the grasp of an esoteric reference or a comprehension of his private symbols that ask from the reader—even the *élite* reader, often the poet-critic—more than he may rightly expect. This is unfortunate because the personality of the man behind the poems is worth cultivating. It is the personality of a cosmopolite who through long and close contact with the world recognizes that, although one cannot withdraw into an ivory tower, there are ways by which one can keep one's finest sensibilities from becoming dulled; who recognizes that in a time when as many panaceas are offered by as many -isms, the solution of life cannot be so simplified. Mr. Stevens sees that only the highest life can bring lasting satisfaction, and he makes a moving appeal to his readers to do their best to inculcate in the mind of the populace a desire for a life of shadows, a desire for the riches that come from an imagination capable of reaching out in all directions to that greater truth that lies beyond the world of fact.

ROBINSON JEFFERS
(1887—   )

THE recent production of Robinson Jeffers' 'free adaptation' of *Medea* with Miss Judith Anderson in the title-rôle has confirmed the opinion of his enthusiastic admirers that Mr. Jeffers is America's greatest living poet—at least her greatest living tragic poet. It is pertinent to attempt to determine whether or not the facts warrant his being placed in this high position. If unwarranted it does Mr. Jeffers more harm than good and will turn the discriminating reader from his work rather than encourage him to enjoy those aspects that deserve high praise. It will recoil, too, on those extravagant critics and reveal their youth and *naïveté*.

Mr. Jeffers is, for example, much admired by Californians for the beauty of his California landscape-painting. What Wordsworth has done for the Lake District, Frost for New England, Shelley for the Italian sky, he, they feel, has done for California, particularly for the Monterey coastal mountain region. Descriptions of this locale are the sole subject of many short poems and provide the setting in which his dramas are played. Nowhere else in his work is he so attuned to his subject-matter. Nothing else is so important to him. 'There is,' he says in 'Contrast,' 'not one memorable person, there is not one mind to stand with the trees, one life with the mountains.'

He is not interested in the veins of a leaf, although he has noticed them. He prefers nature's grander aspects. He is Byron rather than Wordsworth, although at times he seems to share the latter's mystical association with nature. He senses decadence, however, in the quiet English landscape. Only in his Monterey country does he breathe freely. The landscapes of his poems are, one often feels, the chief actors, the chief moulding forces of his characters. He likes high plateaux, whale-backed hills, rock heads and precipitous cliffs, the gorges where they fall to the rocky or sandy shore, and what he calls the mysticism of stone. He rarely admires any of these in their serene and gentle moods, but prefers them licked by the sea-fog, in terrific storms, or on a hot day when the sun burns the water. His sunsets over the sea, like his pictures of the coast itself, are riots of colour, and the mere juxtaposition of colour words from the entire spectrum on vast and awe-inspiring objects plunges the reader into a different world, particularly into a different world of feeling. It is the proper setting for the Manfreds that throng his poems. Even when he describes the 'vast calm vaulting glory of the afterglow' the birds returning to their nests are cormorants. His favourite bird is the hawk. He likes everything it typifies: freedom, wildness, and cruelty. Particularly moving are his pictures of the coming on of night and the moon 'suspended in her great antelope-leap from the head of the cliff.' He prefers 'naked' as an epithet for the moon. He is forced to use extravagant terms to describe extravagant phenomena.

He is aware of the flora and fauna of the region, and a compilation of plant life listed in his poems would be an extensive one. But although a plant never gives a thought that lies too deep for tears it adds to the colour, the form, and the mood he seeks. To achieve his pictorial effects he uses what under normal circumstances would be an excessive number of figures of speech. But as all Californians and most others would agree, the district he describes is not normal. The broad ocean 'burns' like a vast cat's eye, although I have never thought of that quality of a cat's eye. The burning waves are like 'an endless army of horse with banners going by off shore,' the 'fire-maned stars' are like 'stallions in a black pasture, each one with power.' Read quickly, this last simile might impress the reader, but it scarcely bears analysis. The preponderance of images from sex becomes a little fatiguing after a while and the reader begins to turn from the poetry to conjectures about the poet, even in passages that are seemingly objective. Unfortunate though it is, it is often inescapable. When rain is at hand the south wind is invariably 'whetting his knife on the long mountain' and the clouds, usually wild, are flying, or they 'drag,' smoke 'boils' or 'spills,' waves at the river's mouth 'spout up and kill each other.' In quieter times the warm wind is 'wild with fragrance,' and the water is 'burning-glass water' and the still air 'swirls' with heat. A concordance to Mr. Jeffers' work would show, I think, a strong predilection for terms of violence.

But as I have already suggested, these heightened figures, as vague and romantic as any in *Ossian*, create an emotional mood that intensifies the general impact of his long narratives. It is only when the reader has finished and returns to examine the means by which Mr. Jeffers has created his effect that he feels that the means are, or verge on, the meretricious. The twentieth-century Werthers will revel in the emotional orgy made possible, but the serious student of poetry will hesitate before bestowing final approval. He will be forced to admit, however, that Mr. Jeffers has given him a sense of the vastness and grandeur of the California scene.

It is his landscapes that are responsible for the plots of his long poems and for the characters that resolve the plots. However superficially the characters might give the impression of being drawn from life their inspiration is almost wholly literary. He conceals this beneath his over-complicated plots— plots as involved as those in the early Hardy novels. The subject-matter is essentially what Mr. C. S. Lewis would call the 'primary' rather than the 'secondary' material of epic. He is chiefly concerned, that is, with the family rather than with national themes as in the *Æneid* or super-national as in *Paradise Lost*; and then with the family whose members are in bitter conflict. He is concerned with violence rather than with genuine tragedy. This calls for explanation, of course, which will be given in its proper place; but even when he uses the avowedly tragic themes of the Greeks—that of Clytemnestra, Agamemnon, and Cassandra from Æschylus in 'The Tower Beyond Tragedy' or that of the Medea theme from Euripides—he produces melodrama rather than tragedy.

The 'Coast-Range Christ' transplants the Potiphar's wife theme to the Pacific coast and ends violently with the death of the youthful, idealistic David killed by his own father, the hanging of the old husband, and Peace's giving of herself to the sheriff's man. 'Tamar' (see 2 *Samuel* xiii) involves three types of incest besides an illicit love-affair with the man Tamar expects to marry. She finally sets the three men against one another, an idiot aunt sets the house afire, and the poem ends because all the characters are dead. 'The Women at Point Sur' involves some of the same elements— a man's sex relations with an Indian servant, his rape of his daughter, the homosexual relationship between Natalia and Faith, the mother's murder of her child, and the raped daughter's suicide. 'Cawdor' is equally rich in destruction. Here again we meet the Potiphar's wife theme, the murder of the son by the father, the father's Œdipus-like blinding of himself, and other details that complicate the atmosphere of violence. 'Thurso's Landing,' 'Give Your Heart to the Hawks,' and 'Such Counsels You Gave Me' contribute their quotas of fratricide, parricide, paralysing accidents, adultery, hanging, and throat-cutting. Other poems have other crimes, and long before the reader has finished with them he is sur-feited. All and more of the violences of the popular ballads are present without their condensation. His latest volume, *The Double Axe and Other Poems*, differs little from the preceding ones.

Jeffers' characters are devised rather than real. Besides being devised to resolve the intricacies of the plot they are all projections, often compensatory ones, of the poet himself.

His all too obvious lack of any sense of humour permits him to see nothing in its true focus. Distortion rules his pages. His characters are such persons as Mr. Jeffers, had he been born and bred in this isolated region, would have liked to be. His women are wild and free like the hawks with an elemental passion that makes the ordinary episodes of sex in fiction or real life pallid and anaemic. His young heroes are primitive, and strong and willing to fight for their women as viciously as beasts; his older men are patriarchal and resemble the Biblical old men in that retention of their potency past the age when a civilized man is willing to take his warm place in the chimney corner and stroke the cat. His sensitive young idealists succeed in winning nothing but disillusionment and release in death. These latter are probably most nearly Mr. Jeffers.

The reader who fails to see this lack of flesh-and-blood reality of his characters either is careless or lacks an understanding of human nature. They all possess certain basic qualities with which we are familiar, but they are oversimplified. They resemble the 'humorous' characters of Ben Jonson rather than those of Shakespeare, but their range is narrower, and he lacks Jonson's great mass of observed fact. In their darkness they approach those of Webster, Ford, and Tourneur. Jeffers has erred in the same direction as Wordsworth and Hardy in their tendency to find the natural man. Their essential difference is one of nationality and of the consequent different conditioning. The weakness of characterization is more apparent in the men than in the women, although the poet has rather carefully concealed the puppet-strings he so deftly manipulates. His characters fall into well-defined categories. A fierce primitive passion is instinct in California ('Roan Stallion'), Peace O'Farrell ('A Coast-Range Christ'), Tamar ('Tamar'), Fera ('Cawdor'), Fayne ('Give Your Heart to the Hawks'), Helen ('Thurso's Landing'), Faith and Natalia ('The Women at Point Sur'), and Barbara

Howren ('Such Counsels You Gave Me'), with whom we can
contrast the less insistent Michal ('Cawdor'), April ('The
Women at Point Sur'), Clare ('The Loving Shepherdess'), and
France ('Such Counsels'). Lee Cauldwell, Lance Fraser
('Give Your Heart to the Hawks'), and Reave Thurso
('Thurso's Landing'), reveal the strong male tactics of fiction,
and occasional fact. Will Andrews ('Tamar'), David Carrow
('The Coast-Range Christ'), Hood Cawdor ('Cawdor'),
Michael ('Give Your Heart'), and Rick Armstrong ('Thurso's
Landing') are the willing or unwilling victims of women's
lust. The fathers in Mr. Jeffers' poems are (as I have men-
tioned) patriarchal in their attempts to rule their families.

However diverse the manifestations of violence may be, it is
Jeffers' women that appal the reader. He becomes particularly conscious of the intensification of light and shade,
or, to borrow a term from art criticism, of the jamming of
the shadows in his portraits of highly passionate women who
typify the extreme degree of the life force. (See Shaw, *Man
and Superman*, for the comic operation of this force.)

Jeffers seems to admire Fayne, Fera, Tamar, and others,
but is it not possible that he also subconsciously hates them
with an intensity that overshadows any possible conscious
admiration? He admires them because more than any of his
other characters they offer the most complete rebellion from
the mass-man he so thoroughly despises. Euripides may put
into the mouth of his characters diatribes against women,
as, for example, 'neither land or sea produces a race so
pestilent' as woman (*Hecuba*); or Andromache's 'though
some god hath devised cures for mortals against the venom of
reptiles, no man ever yet hath discovered aught to cure a
woman's venom, which is far worse than viper's sting or
scorching flame; so terrible a curse are we to mankind'
(*Andromache*). Compared with Jeffers' presentation of women,
however, Euripides is mild-mannered and courtly. It is strange
that no psychoanalyst has explored this phase of Jeffers.

It is frequently pleasant to turn to these elemental characters in their primitive family conflicts as an antidote to the opposite extreme of over-subtilization practised by so many modern poets. It is as bad to persist in futile explorings of the subconscious to the exclusion of a normal point of view as it is to attempt to look at life to-day from the point of view of the Greek dramatists. Actually, of course, the point of view of Mr. Jeffers is less harmful than its opposite, although Plato would certainly have banned him from his republic. It would also be a mistake, in spite of his frequent use of Greek themes, to think that he has caught the Greek spirit. The powerful impression made on a young person of restricted emotional experience may carry over into emotional maturity; but his own experience will prove a corrective. He will gradually realize that this vicariously induced experience does not coincide with reality. He will prefer less jamming of the shadows. If he continues to read Mr. Jeffers it will be for other reasons than the progress of the narrative or a study of character. That Mr. Jeffers has himself been able to continue so long in this unrelieved vein can only result from his having so studiously isolated himself from people. His point of view is essentially youthful, and he simply does not understand what true tragedy is.

In order to understand the paradox in Mr. Jeffers it is necessary to have some general concept of his attitude toward life. He believes that professed Christianity with its doctrine of love for the common man is dangerous. It is, he says, the degradation of life and its eventual dissolution. 'The Apes of Christ lift up their hands to praise love,' but the present saviour of mankind is 'wisdom without love.' More important is 'power without hatred, mind like a many-bladed machine subduing the world with deep indifference.' Pity is unnecessary; love is dangerous because it is a clever servant, and insufferable master, and the trap that caught Christ ('Shine Perishing Republic'). Humanity, he adds elsewhere, 'is the mould to break away from, the crust to break through, the coal to break into fire, the atom to be split.' Because peace is such a personal, unique quality, he who has found it for himself cannot help others to find it. The masses will find salvation in death; all each can do while he lives is to 'make his health in his mind, to love the coast opposite humanity' ('Meditation on Saviors').

When Jeffers rationalizes on the basis that what is true for him must be true for all, he goes off on a tangent. Civilization becomes for him a transient sickness, and people in cities—the greatest victims of this illness—are anxious to be human again ('New Mexican Mountain'). Whether or not people in the cities are the greatest victims is a debatable question and we need only turn to the people in *North of Boston* for a possible refutation. Jeffers is not the only contemporary poet, however, to hold such an opinion. Less questionable is Jeffers' general attitude toward mankind, although even here he takes the extreme point of view; because each of us is, as he says, 'caught in the stone of his own person.' I can only partially agree that our blood 'is rather ignoble in its quiet times, mean in its pleasure, slavish in the mass; but at stricken moments it can shine terrible against the dark magnificence of things' ('Thurso's Landing'). The dignity of death has ever been impressive.

Where some see progress, Jeffers sees decay. Our rapidly expanding consciousness of empire is the decay that will lead America to dissolution. To avert that dissolution he would have man return to vision, desire, unnatural crime, inhuman science, wild love—all of which would 'slit eyes in the mask' ('Roan Stallion'). The 'communal people' do not know 'the wild God of the world.' The hawk, however, remembers and with the blue-heron and the red-shafted woodpecker 'live their felt natures; they know their norm and live it to the brim; they understand life. While men moulding themselves to the anthill have choked their natures until their souls die in them; they have sold themselves for protection.' Such people are 'fractional' with no centre 'but in the eyes and mouths that surround them, having no function but to serve and support civilization, the enemy of man.' After further excoriation, he finally admits, however, that 'it is barely possible that even men's present lives are something' ('The Broken Balance'). It is interesting to observe that both Jeffers and Wallace Stevens see the populace in essentially the same light. But to repair the disaster, each would take his position at a pole opposite to the other.

Jeffers has little sympathy with those who would escape the pain of life. No person's pain is unique, but 'all that lives was maimed and bleeding, caged or in blindness' and he sees life greater than 'its functions,' and its 'accidents more important than its pains and pleasures' ('Cawdor'). Or as he elsewhere says, 'Praise life, it deserves praise, but the praise of life that forgets the pain is a pebble rattled in a dry gourd' ('Praise Life'). Mr. Jeffers' most eloquent appeal for the sufferance of pain is Fayne's plea to her husband Lance after he has killed his brother:

> I know you are strong enough
> To give your heart to the hawks without a cry
> And bear it in lovely silence to the end of life.
> What else do you want? Ah. Confession's a coward
> Running to officers, begging help.
> 'Give Your Heart to the Hawks'

Earlier in the poem Mr. Jeffers regrets what he feels to be over-anguish for the death of Lance's brother. Neither drunkenness nor murder are 'enormous evils,' because, as he philosophizes,

> For all delight he has lost, pain has been saved him;
> And the balance is strangely perfect,
> And why are you pale with misery?

Because you have saved him from foolish labors and all
   the vain days?
From desires denied and desires staled with attaining,
And from fear of want, and from all diseases, and from fear
   of death?
Or because you have kept him from becoming old,
When the teeth drop and the eyes dim and the ears grow
   dull,
And the man is ashamed?
Surely it is nothing worse to be slain in the overflowing
Than to fall in the emptiness.

Is this not sentimentality rather than sound thinking? Is it
not a defeatist, nihilistic attitude toward life? Are not the
fears imaginary and baseless?

Jeffers' first two volumes were idealistic, optimistic, and
traditional, but the complete about-face can be easily ex-
plained. Like so many emotionally unstable young men of
promise of the early twenties he suffered disillusionment in the
era following the first World War, a disillusionment from
which he has never recovered. He found a certain measure of
personal peace by withdrawing to the Monterey coast where
he proceeded to construct a world of his own. Forced to
reject mass-man he has compensated by focusing his attention
on those qualities which to him carry the mark of permanence.
Having so low an opinion of his contemporaries he has made
posterity his goal, to attain which he has been sedulous in
seeking those subjects where life 'was purged of its ephemeral
accretions.' His inspiration, as I have already noted, has been
essentially literary: Greek tragedy, the Bible, a footnote in a
Scott novel, the sagas, the ballads, to name but a few. He has
transplanted these seeds to the California coast and has sought
to naturalize them.

His later poetry is largely the product of an outraged
idealism, an attitude of mind now out of fashion. Because of

this persistent view of the world the mature reader finds himself out of sympathy with his philosophy, although it still strikes a responsive chord in the emotionally young of any age. Far nobler, I think, than the person who to save himself isolates himself, is the person who learns to walk with dignity through the crowds, uncorrupted by them; one whose nobility is not rusted by contact with dank souls.

The mature reader, although he may be carried along by Mr. Jeffers' often powerful rhetoric, will not be deceived by it, especially if he is at pains to analyse it. To achieve his effects he uses everything except rhyme, which he early discarded. Figures of speech thickly stud his work, similes and metaphors being applied with so lavish a hand that one is reminded of a young poet at work rather than an artist who has learned to use his ornamentation sparingly. Passages abound in which every line contains a metaphor or simile. Brief comment has already been made of their use in his nature pictures. His characters inspire a further horde of figures. Fayne's cinnabar-coloured hair, for example, is like 'a flag of life against the pale east'; Cawdor's young wife is 'as silent as a sheathed knife'; and Mr. Howren in his death agony inspires an inexcusable suspended simile of seven lines in which he is compared to a 'powerfully organized state in the agony of insurrection.' Subtlety is absent and rightly so. Mr. Jeffers seeks the larger effects, and from the point of view of the general reader, probably finds them, although the serious student of poetry remains unimpressed. Metaphors, too, are thickly strewn throughout the poems. Those arising from implied biological comparisons are scientifically accurate. When he speaks of Miss Howren's face as being 'basilisk-pale,' he obviously seeks a purely literary and emotional rather than pictorial reaction.

Unless, however, one is alert, these smaller elements are felt rather than seen. They are like certain instruments in a symphony that give body to the massed effect, but are blended to form a new instrument of rich colour. They are lost in the surging of his long line, his unique contribution to modern poetry.

In Mr. Jeffers' earliest volumes he used traditional verse-patterns which he discarded simultaneously with his early idealism. In 'The Coast-Range Christ' he employs an eight-stress couplet with only minor success. Soon, however, he practically abandoned rhyme and developed the long un-rhymed line that he has often used with outstanding effectiveness; often but not invariably. Too frequently this line degenerates into prose, and were it printed as such, few would suspect from its inner tension that it was meant to be anything else. He sought a rhythmic line 'moulded more closely to the subject' than was the older English poetry. The rhythm came from many sources: 'physics, biology, beat of blood, the tidal environments of life.'

Obviously, generalizations give only a partial picture. In 'Tamar,' for example, he uses two general patterns of lines. Some sections, as I scan them, are predominantly five-stress lines with the frequent interpolation of one of six stresses; others are in a much longer line—twice as long, in fact—and vary between ten and twelve stresses. The line of the 'Coast-Range Christ' has regularly eight stresses. Those of 'Cawdor,' 'The Women at Point Sur,' 'Such Counsels You Gave Me,' and others vary from five to twelve. The feet within the lines are likewise irregular. Actually, the rhythms do not vary greatly from prose rhythms. They are essentially those of rhetoric.

Naturally, Mr. Jeffers is enough of a poet to realize that he must compensate for this freedom, and he generally does. He makes frequent use of repetition and alliteration. He not only repeats single words, but larger units. In 'Tamar,' for example, he controls the reader's reaction by repeating with slight variants and at irregularly-spaced intervals the half-line, 'Came down the river and straggled through the wood to the sea.' In the repetitions he substitutes 'wandered' for 'straggled.'

This is an effective line for his long poems. It is, however, ill-adapted for short poems. It lacks the time to gather momentum. For this reason, I think the shorter poems less effective than the long. These shorter poems, also, being generally of a more reflective or purely descriptive nature, lack the energetic epithets that in the longer poems compensate for their great freedom of form.

Frankly, however, I think Mr. Jeffers' long line detracts from rather than adds to the tragic effect he seeks. He provides us with melodrama rather than tragedy. To be successful the violence of his subject-matter must be compensated for by a rigid control of his verse. This he fails to do. After reading most of the long narratives and before turning to his 'free adaptation' of *Medea*, I believed I could foretell the course he would follow. To refresh my memory I reread a literal translation of Euripides' great play and then turned to the new version. I found what I expected. He had altered some of the main qualities of Creon's character, he removed the restraining force of the measured verse and substituted his own. He shortened and broke up many of the speeches and he ended by sacrificing depth for speed. Whether intentionally or otherwise he deprived the characters of their tragic stature. He made the play suitable for a Broadway production, but he did it by emasculating Euripides.

What he has done to this great tragedy gives us a clue to him as an artist and as a man. As an artist, he lacks a true grasp of form, that careful integration of subject, imagery, and prosody that results in a strong aesthetic impact, that makes us realize that for a moment we have seen life whole. 'Dear Judas,' for example, is not clearly enough realized; its outline is vague and troubled. The same is true of 'The Women at Point Sur,' 'Roan Stallion,' and others. Many have professed surprise to learn that as a man his private life is that of a

I

mild-mannered, scholarly, kindly man, albeit one that shuns the life of the cities and prefers solitude. It would be more surprising to find him otherwise. It is the rigidly self-disciplined or timid persons who frequently revolt via their imaginations into the realms of violence. Mr. Jeffers admits as much. The poem dealing with Ferguson is, he says, 'in some ways my very self but mostly my antipodes' ('For Una').

'Permanent things are,' he says, 'what is needful in a poem' ('Point Joe'), 'things temporally of great dimension.' And elsewhere, 'The pallid pursuit of the world's beauty on paper, unless a tall angel comes to require it, is a pitiful pastime' ('Second-Best'). Aware of what is needful, it is unfortunate that Mr. Jeffers has not succeeded. Too often the tall angel has failed to come and he has found himself bored with the long poem he was writing. He was not only bored with the violence he described but also expressed the wish that 'any sweet soul that reads it' will also be bored ('For Una'). It requires no sweet soul to share his boredom.

What his isolation gave him in one way it took from him in another. He detached himself from the important things of earth at the moment he sought to come closer to earth. His work can never be thought of as a reading of life. In seeking the permanent he has missed it. Had he had the saving grace of humour he might have been more successful, but in the writing of no poet of genuine importance are there less visible signs of humour, that saving grace which enables a man to see himself in perspective. Mr. Jeffers takes himself far too seriously. On the other hand, were he not always so intensely serious his rhetoric would degenerate into burlesque. 'The Women at Point Sur' is only narrowly saved from such a fate.

Being humourless himself he imagines that the characters he has created have life. To me they are shadowy creations that fade almost as soon as born. The pleasure derived from his work is that of immediate excitement like that of a 'thriller'

or a professional wrestling match. Only when it is over does
the observer realize that he has been hoaxed. This judgment
applies, of course, to his long poems. Unfortunately, I find his
short poems dull. They present a point of view of life with
which I have little sympathy. He does not compensate for
the uncongeniality of his subject-matter, as does Mr. Eliot, by
presenting those ideas in a form that induces a willing suspension of disbelief. He will undoubtedly continue to be popular
with a certain type of audience. But it is an audience incapable
of grasping the fact that Mr. Jeffers' reading of life is myopic,
even pathological.

ARCHIBALD MACLEISH
(1892—   )

PART I

MR. ARCHIBALD MACLEISH is an important poet of the middle generation of modern American poets. His first volume meriting attention appeared in 1925. He had, it is true, published two volumes before this— *Songs For a Summer's Day* (1915) and *Tower of Ivory* (1917)— but these are juvenile verses and devoid of the intellectual content which an early mentor felt to animate them. We can dismiss them as Mr. MacLeish has done.

Many persons are inclined to look upon Mr. MacLeish as the Joseph Addison of the New Deal. Such an attitude focuses attention on one small phase of his work, and that the least important from the point of view of his stature as a poet.

It is true that his most insistent subject is political, but he is not political in the party sense of the word, but in its larger connotation of the problem of man's relation to society. Other subjects, however, are equally important from the point of view of his survival as a poet. These are the subjects that concern every poet at some stage of his poetic life: autobiographic reminiscences, love, nature, the consciousness of and attempted solution of his aesthetic problems, and miscellaneous subjects. A better insight into his treatment of his materials would be their grouping as nostalgic, contemplative, and active; or into poems of feeling and poems of the intellect. But to divide into compartments is to abstract and deprive.

The autobiographic poems—and I exclude those on love—

deal with childhood and gradually maturing reminiscences; those of a sensitive boy, as in 'Eleven,' a poem difficult to discuss because its significance is in its feeling; of a developing youth, as in 'Cook County,' the place where he grew up; of a young man, as in 'L'an Trentiesme de mon Aage,' which records the gradual maturing of the poet; in 'Le Secret Humain,' in which he realizes that he will understand the secret of man's being after death; and in 'Memorial Rain' and its later complement of disillusion, 'Lines for an Interment.' Of all these 'Memorial Rain' is the most successful. By the juxtaposition of the memorial words of the ambassador dedicating an American cemetery in Brussels, with the description of the gathering storm, and then the rain on the grave of the person dear to him, Mr. MacLeish communicates a deep sense of personal bereavement. Particularly interesting is the heightened emotion contributed by the final eight lines.

Less assignable to specific experiences, yet far removed from the abstract, are the poems on nature. 'Immortal Autumn,' more rhetorical than Keats' ode on the same subject, shows, however, as great a love for that golden season. But it would give an incomplete picture of the poet's love for nature to overlook its influence on his images and its background value in numerous poems. 'Memory Green' has almost the Frostian quality of 'The Tuft of Flowers' without in any specific way resembling it. It communicates the feeling common to sensitive persons of having previously shared the beauty of the moment, whether it be a view of the hills or of the moon, and deriving therefrom a modicum of immortality or of an intensified aesthetic experience ('Pony Rock,' 'Nocturne,' 'Selene Afterwards,' 'The Farm').

Mr. MacLeish, like Hardy, seems to be more interested in the reverse side of love than in its positive qualities. But at no time does he approach Hardy's subtlety of analysis. In one of his better poems on the subject ('Against Illuminations') he recognizes that what we love is not the girl herself, but the

projection of our love on her. When he does praise the
beloved, however, he does it in a modern key and in the spirit
of revolt from the traditional sonneteers ('Not Marble in the
Gilded Monuments'). He recognizes, too, like Arnold with
a difference, that when liberty, pride, and hope vanish—
heretofore men's guides—love alone remains ('Pole Star for
this Year'). The poems dealing with the less happy aspects
of love are in general more effective than those of a more
favourable tone, and probably because the inherent drama in
them is greater. Even these, however, fail to communicate
a sense of appreciable depth ('Broken Promise,' 'Before
March,' 'De Votre Bonheur etc.'). Some of the finest poems
in this genre are in the sequence 'The Woman on the Stair,'
strongly reminiscent in plot of Meredith's 'Modern Love.'
Since their distinction lies in their technical qualities, their
discussion is delayed to Part II.

Except for 'You, Andrew Marwell,' 'The Pat of Earth,'
'Conquistador,' and perhaps one or two others, the poems in
Poems: 1924–1933 are the weakest because of their too frequent
stress on the obvious. 'Verses for a Centennial,' 'March,'
and 'Men of My Century Loved Mozart,' among others,
detract rather than add to Mr. MacLeish's stature. From 'The
Pat of Earth,' originally published in 1925, Mr. MacLeish has
deleted several passages in the version found in *Poems:
1924–1933*. The general effect of the deletions is a tightening
of the poetry at the expense of clarity. As it stands, however,
it is a good poem and illustrates a fact, elsewhere negatively
supported, that when confronted with a muscular idea, the
poet can handle it. He has made a happy fusion of a modern
American setting with the old ritual of the Gardens of Adonis,
which had as its purpose the insuring of fertility of women as
well as of grain. The poem, impressionistic in the manner of
The Waste Land, details the maturing of the young girl, her
ripening, marriage, childbirth, death, and the assurance of
the continuity of life through her children. The poet moves

deftly from the symbolism of the Adonis cult to its present manifestation in the mystery of life.

'Conquistador' is, to me, an overpraised poem. It is needlessly obscure and remains so even with subsequent readings. If the reader turns from the poem itself to Bernal de Diaz' *The True History of the Conquest of Mexico* (Keatinge translation, 2 vols., New York, 1927), he immediately realizes that the obscurities are the poet's and not those of his source. Often the telescoping of events, the too abrupt breaks between books, the paucity of materials make any strong unified aesthetic import impossible. Then, also, the too frequent occurrence of broken lines, partial thoughts, and the over-use of dots distract and annoy the reader. At times, fortunately, the story grips the poet so strongly that he stirs the reader profoundly. Books six and seven are good, and eight to ten are excellent. In this latter section the poem sweeps and rises steadily to the end, holding the reader in its grasp with its speed, forward movement, and imperceptible concentrating force.

It is as a political poet, however, that Mr. MacLeish is at his best. I do not include in this category his verse plays designed for radio production such as *Panic*, *The Fall of the City*, *America Was Promises*, and *Air Raid*, or his verse complement to the photographic commentary of America, *Land of the Free*. These belong in a separate category and cannot be judged by the same standards as the poems with less obvious propagandist intentions. Strict chronology is unimportant. An attempt at an orderly discussion of his thought, however, soon discovers that the poet is not static and that the farthest reaches of his political thought coincide with his latest periods of composition.

Although inclined to believe that nothing is at the end of the world, the poet realizes the impossibility of running away from life. But does he find some meaning to life in this complex world? He is aware of the waste land, he is unable to accept traditional religion, and he senses that we can never know ourselves. We must learn, then, to accept life without understanding it.[1] The resolution of the conflicting elements one constantly encounters not only presents a problem to the poet, but is a resolution not often solved. Mr. MacLeish attempts it in 'The Hamlet of A. MacLeish,' inspired, I believe, by his awareness of Shakespeare's solution of a similar contemporary problem in his *Hamlet*. Shakespeare has, for example, he says, 'reduced to poetic order and made recognizable the common experience of his age. He has shown how the conflict of appearance and reality which give *Hamlet* its dramatic tension relates to the conflict of appearance and reality characteristic of the thinking of his time. . . . Shakespeare's play is such an organization of the moral confusion and intellectual anxiety of his contemporaries as a great poet can accomplish; and Hamlet remains to our day the one figure in which we recognize the experience of intellectual doubt at that extremest point where doubt is no longer possible and only belief can be supported. . . . What is really remarkable about the experience of our generation is the fact that no comparable organization of the public yet private life of our time has been attempted by contemporary poetry ('Poetry and the Public World,' in *A Time to Speak*, pp. 89, 90).

In Shakespeare's day it was the struggle between the Ptolemaic and the Copernican systems of the universe. To-day it is between the traditional and the Einsteinian, and the problem of what we are remains a riddle even though we can split atoms ('Einstein'). Because the poet's experiences with these riddles stir him to intense and personal emotions the expression resolves itself into excellent poetry.

Mr. MacLeish makes his public avowal of a change from aesthetic to political interests in a series of poems more rhetorical than basically poetic ('Sentiments for a Dedication' and 'Yacht for Sale'). Using the image of a yacht as a symbol

---

[1] 'The End of the World,' 'Tourist Death,' 'Lines for a Prologue,' 'The Seafarer.'

for his youth, he acknowledges that it was 'frail at the keel
And too sharp in the bow.' He reproves the poets of the past
for having concerned themselves with kings and aristocratic
matters rather than with the democratic—the life and ways of
the common man—because he sees that man's constant hope
and upward struggle is 'grave, noble and tragic' ('Reproach
to Dead Poets,' 'Men'). He is at his best in such poems as
the patriotic 'American Letter.' Aware of the homogeneity
of the people of France or Italy, he regrets this lack in
America—'dressed as one—no brothers among them'—
because it gives us the sense of being anchorless. In spite of
that, however, we must face the fact that it is only in America
that we can have any real being. Granted that America has
been exploited by men like Morgan, Mellon, and other so-
called 'Makers' of America; despoilers rather—

> They screwed her scrawny and gaunt with their seven-year
>   panics:
> They bought her back on their mortgages old-whore-cheap:
> They fattened their bonds at her breasts till the thin blood
>   ran from them:

> Men have forgotten how full clear and deep
> The Yellowstone moved on the gravel and grass grew
> When the land lay waiting for her westward people!
>   'Frescoes for Mr. Rockefeller's City'

There remains, however, her deep-seated vitality that has
exerted such a profound influence on the different nationalities
in the melting-pot.

We must recognize, he continues, that it is useless to take
a nostalgic backward look at the seeming security and solidity
of our ancestors when political changes were imperceptible.
We can only look forward, even though life is too fluid for
our desires ('Land's End,' '1933'). Class distinctions must
not narrow our vision. We should love excellence wherever

found, because otherwise 'we cheat ourselves in cheating worth of wonder.' Man must realize that it takes courage to force the world to give us what we are justified in demanding of it. Too many, unfortunately, cannot face such facts. They are optimists only so long as they are the 'haves' in an unchanging society, but they become strangely silent when confronted with the necessity for a change of political thinking; they emulate the flies who freeze and numbly accept the coming on of winter rather than attempting to emulate the hawks who, unperturbed, dominate the situation, however sharp the struggle ('Speech to the Detractors,' 'Speech to a Crowd,' 'The Lost Speakers,' 'Poem for a Time of Change').

Other phases of Mr. MacLeish's political thinking are more baldly stated in his documentary *Land of the Free* (1938) and in his verse plays for radio: *Panic* (1935), *The Fall of the City* (1937), *Air Raid* (1938), and *America Was Promises* (1939). In these, Mr. MacLeish sacrifices in great measure his concept of the poet as enunciated in his 'Invocation to the Social Muse' and does those things which by so doing will, he realized, cause him to be soon forgotten. As poetry these are weak when placed alongside his best work and lack its contemplative quality. Since they have prosodic interest, let us reserve them for consideration when we examine his technical achievement.

PART II

In his 'Ars Poetica' Mr. MacLeish mentions that 'a poem should be equal to: not true' and that it 'should not mean, but be.' Since his lasting quality as well as present stature depends upon his ability to make a poem 'be,' let us review some of the methods used for creating this state of being. His earliest poems are in every respect traditional in the manner of the Georgians, particularly Rupert Brooke, of whom there are innumerable echoes. This is to be expected since Brooke was at the height of his popularity in 1915 and

1916, particularly at Yale. The diction, imagery, and verse-patterns of this early work have little originality; at best they reveal a sensitive ear. In the work of the immediate post-war years and, in fact, until fairly recently, Mr. MacLeish attempted to give greater strength to his verse in the same way as the novelists like Hemingway and Dos Passos—by the use of strong Anglo-Saxon four- or five-letter words. He uses these words, however, with a self-conscious air and calls attention to them in a manner that one would not do in whose vocabulary they are at home. Instead, therefore, of these words investing the poem with greater masculinity, they have the opposite effect. On the whole, however, his vocabulary is simple and direct and becomes increasingly so in his later work, in spite of such aberrations as 'cooked dough' when he obviously means bread.

Alliteration is a stylistic device which, instead of subtly controlling his communication, frequently draws attention to itself. This I found to be particularly true in 'Conquistador.' Generally, however, it is integrated in the poem, and, at times, happily combined with repetition, as on 's' in 'They think how the sound of the surf is the sound of forever.' He rather likes this trick and we find it not only in such lines as 'In love not live there never are two lovers' ('The Woman on the Stair,' vi), but on a larger scale faintly echoing Eliot's 'Ash Wednesday':

> I have forgotten you. There is a grey light on my
> Hands and I have forgotten you. There is light enough.
> There is light enough left to forget your face by—
> Voice by: to forget you. As long as the
> Light lasts on my hands I forget you.
> There needs be some light; a little.
>
> *Ibid.*, viii

Unfortunately, however, such lines, devoid of inner tension, have little survival value.

Repetition not only serves to give form to the parts of a poem, but to a whole poem. Frequently, he will begin and end the poem with the same words. In 'The Farm,' for example, a poem that reveals his mastery of prosody, he begins and ends with the question, 'Why do you listen trees?' Repetition can be, however, too self-conscious as in 'and he ate simnel And sweet cakes he ate and a kind of partridges.'

Mr. MacLeish makes an abundant use of similes, many of which are not readily grasped in a first reading. This, of course, is not a fault. The fault lies in his too easy ones; those that are too much on the surface, that come too readily to hand. His metaphors are apt to be tighter. Birds, particularly the strong-winged hawks, and gulls, ships, and the sea fascinate him and furnish his best figures. In this he resembles Robinson Jeffers. 'The Sunset Piece' is a sustained metaphor in which the ship is the earth and the present 'the squall of time.' He captures the quality of a snow-storm in such lines as 'the white unable wandering of the air Whirled everywhere' ('The Woman on the Stair,' iii). 'Unable' is a happy choice. More effective than any set of figures for capturing the mood is his selection of telling details, as in the following picture of spring.

> With haste: with the haggard color:
> With Shad-blow:[1] plum blossoms (Multitudes)
> Came and again spring
> Sole on a bush: single in
> Apple branches: tasteless:
> Filling the low places as
> Water in flood fills them:
> Leaving blossomless hills.
>
> 'The Woman on the Stair,' i

Mr. MacLeish is most original as a poet in his stanzaic

[1] Shad: common name for shadbush, a shrublike tree producing numerous white flowers in early spring; not to be confused with flowering dogwood.

innovations. Here one finds his greatest sensitivity, the finest expression of a subtle and delicate ear, the deepest insight into the poet's innermost soul. His first major contribution derives from the *terza rima* of Dante. Instead of rhyme, he substitutes assonance. For convenience's sake let us dub this *terza assonanza.* His most sustained use of the form (although he is not here slavishly tied to it) is in 'Conquistador.' It is admirably suited to narrative and is capable of speed, forward movement, and possesses an imperceptible concentrating force. At other times it takes on the quality of ritual, or the reader unconsciously thinks of the movement of Eliot's 'The Journey of the Magi.' It is one of his most recurring prosodic patterns and often his most successful. He also uses assonance in couplets ('Frescoes for Mr. Rockefeller's City,' 'American Letter,' and others) and in quatrains ('Frescoes, etc., 1'). In 'The Sunset Piece' he goes one step farther, having lines one and three in assonance and two and four in rhyme. Half-rhymes (consonance)—lake-like, far-for, vine-vane, altogether-to gather, west-waste—are largely responsible for the effect in 'Cook County.' Or, he may eschew rhyme or assonance in his stanza-patterns, depending on his purpose ('Men').

I think he has been primarily concerned in his experiments in finding that prosodic pattern which best reflects the temper of our contemporary life. It may be the rhythm of a popular song, as in 'Frescoes, etc., 5,' or a somewhat syncopated jazz rhythm as in those instances when the accent falls unexpectedly. In 'Cinema of a Man,' the first two lines of each stanza will illustrate what I mean:

The earth is bright through the bows of the moon like a
    dead planet
It is silent it has no sound the sun is on it
It shines . . .

He sits in the rue St. Jacques at the iron table
It is dusk it is growing cold the roof stone glitters on the
     gable
The taxis . . .

Now he sits on the porch of the Villa Serbelloni
He is eating white bread and brown honey
The sun is hot . . .

Or it may be a different rhythmical effect, as in 'The Lost
Speakers' and '"Dover Beach"—a note to that poem.' By
placing unaccented articles and prepositions—'the,' 'a,' and
'of'—at the end of a line he subtly produces in the mind of
the reader, almost without his awareness, the effect of the
pause just before a wave breaks on the shore, followed by the
water's retreat over the shingle:

> After forty a man's a fool to wait in the
> sea's face for the full force and the roaring of
> surf to come over him: droves of careening water.

As important as any of these more obvious prosodic devices
is the poet's use of falling rhythms, prominent in many of
the already cited poems. He attempts to achieve the quality
of American speech which he feels *descends from* stressed
syllables, rather than *rising toward* them. This is not a discovery
of Mr. MacLeish, however, as any student of metric is aware.
It has long been recognized that to avoid complicated ter-
minology in the discussion of modern prosody it has been
almost necessary to employ the amphibrach ($\cup/\cup$) and the
paeon,[1] the third paeon ($\cup\cup/\cup$) being the most frequently
used. Hardy used both extensively. Actually, I think, Hardy
achieves what would be a closer approximation to American
speech, and without meaning to do so, than does MacLeish,
and he does so by a judicious mixture of iambs and anapests
with frequent third paeons. I do not think the differences

---

[1] Paeon: a foot of four syllables, one long and three short, called *first, second, third* or
fourth paeon, according as the long syllable stood first, second, etc.

between American and English speech-rhythms as basic as MacLeish thinks them to be.

While on the subject of speech-rhythms let us look for a moment at his verse plays which have given him a wider public than would otherwise be conscious of his work. In *Panic* (1935) he set out deliberately to capture what he felt to be the qualities of American speech: rhythms 'nervous not muscular; excited, not deliberate; vivid, not proud.' What he actually achieved was the type of bastard speech-rhythms that our ears are deluged with when we turn on the radio. Even in the 'soap-operas'[1] the slightest remark is spoken with bated breath. This artificiality reaches its ultimate in Norman Corwin's *On a Note of Triumph*, a work which to me is the epitome of bad taste and the rankest fustian. Fortunately, Mr. MacLeish is never guilty of such things. Actually, of course, most of *Panic* is not a five-stress verse with syllables varying from five to fifteen or seventeen that approaches speech-rhythms. The speeches of McGafferty, the bankers and the blind man are in these verse patterns, but the choruses of people are in three- or four-stressed verse and a highly artificial verse at that. I find the play confusing in its aim and it can never be anything except a *tour de force*. It hammers too consistently in a staccato manner, and I do not feel that the author has clearly resolved his thesis in the terms of the theatre. What is true of *Panic* is likewise true of *Air Raid* (1938) with its scherzo-like quality of immediacy rather than contemplation, and even more true of *America Was Promises* (1939). These with *The Fall of the City* (1937) and the document-ary *Land of the Free* (1938) must be judged from their effectiveness as propaganda and not as poetry. They, therefore, largely lie outside the province of this essay. All of them, I think, would be effective on the radio where the listeners would grasp the message through their feelings rather than their intellect.

I mentioned in connection with 'Conquistador' that Mr. Mac-

[1] See note on p. 3.

Leish is apt to obscure his communication by broken sentences and the over-use of dots. He provides the spring-board, but the reader must judge the depth of the water from the dots. It is the same as blind-diving, never a comfortable pastime. He makes this same over-use in many of the shorter poems. He further needlessly confuses the reader by the absence of punctuation. 'Immortal Autumn' is a case in point. What does he gain by the omission of semicolons and periods at the fourteen strong stops besides the omission of commas at the lesser stops? I cannot believe that he is like the young English poet (was it Auden, Spender, or MacNeice?) who omitted them because he didn't know where to put them in.

Many influences are evident in his work. That of Mr. T. S. Eliot is too evident. Not only one or two, but almost every well-known poem of his is definitely echoed in some poem or other of Mr. MacLeish. This is natural but unfortunate. Mr. MacLeish has shown himself capable of writing poetry that is so complete a fusion of his influences that we have a new voice. It is in such work that we must expect to find the qualities of permanence. In many ways he is at a crucial point in his career—that point when the domination of the sensuous yields to the domination of the intellect. Will he, as Yeats and Mr. Frost have done, so blend and fuse these elements that his later poetry will be the natural outgrowth of his earlier; or will he make a sharp dichotomy? His more recent works would indicate that perhaps he is confused in his own mind as to the true function of a poet, or, if not that, as to what sort of audience he wishes for himself. He cannot serve two masters. True enough, several of his prose utterances ('In Challenge, not Defence,' 'Public Speech and Private Speech in Poetry,' 'Poetry and the Public World') reveal his attempt to solve the dichotomy in his own mind. He should remember, however, that time has already given us the best answer in the poems that have survived, and he knows the answer—'a poem should not mean, but be.'

E. E. CUMMINGS
(1894—   )

MR. E. E. CUMMINGS has been before the public for more than twenty-five years, yet in no poet writing over so long a time is there so little change. Qualities of adolescence apparent in his early work still exist in his latest work, both in his subject-matter and its treatment. Technical novelties that startled his early readers and beguiled them into thinking of him as a revolutionary writer have become a part of his regular stock-in-trade. Because time has revealed that they are technical swagger and nothing more, they now annoy the adult reader rather than beguile. It is unfortunate that this is so, because Mr. Cummings frequently reveals genuine poetic qualities.

The cause for his failure to develop into a truly significant poet rather than to continue as an anachronistic survival of an important epoch in American poetry is everywhere manifest in the subject-matter of his verse. He was a sensitive young idealist aware of the beauty of the world of nature about him, but also keenly aware of its ugliness, an ugliness which caused so deep a revulsion in him that he either turned from it completely or, forcing himself to look at it, distorted it out of all perspective. His so-called realistic poems are in essence poems of reverse idealism. Like so many of his generation he took the easy way out and sought to escape by running away. It is one thing to get away from a too-familiar scene in order to see it in better perspective; it is quite another to get away in order to forget the scene. To try to escape by running away is one of the most certain ways to commit moral suicide.

In his poems that are purely autobiographic, in those that

K

capture an isolated moment of pure beauty, in his far too
numerous poems on love in which he is apt to confuse the act
of coitus with love, and in his so-called realistic portraits of
the New York scene, we are everywhere confronted by an
adolescent attitude of mind. He seems to find it a matter for
regret that the poet must travel a lonely road and be a misunderstood individual. The poet is not unique in this; every
person not content with mediocrity at some time or other in
his life adjusts himself to this fact. Loneliness, however,
need not—should not, in fact—be confused with unhappiness.

Many of the poems in *Tulips and Chimneys* succeed in isolat-
ing moments of pure beauty by impressionistic means. I for
one, however, sense a lack of muscularity in these and feel
that in a world such as ours in which Mr. Cummings reached
his majority, such an attitude is an anachronism. He is too
much out of the stream of life for his work to have significance. He tends toward preciosity, and the sense of conscious
superiority imparted to the reader becomes intolerable.
He reveals himself too much concerned with himself rather
than with what he might be able to do about those things to
which he objects. He expatriates himself only to assume a
disdainful attitude toward those of his fellow-countrymen
better able financially to enjoy the pleasures of Europe. Often
he gives the impression of a tortured, neurotic soul, afraid to
face reality. He attempts to hide this fear beneath an assumed
air of superiority. Because he has run away he has given
himself no chance to draw strength from that soil which can
alone succour him—his native soil.

The reader must not mistake Mr. Cummings for an intellectual poet. He is almost entirely a creature of the senses, who
is constantly striving to attain a greater realization of himself
through the senses. Or to borrow his own words: 'Myself
surveys safely the complete important profane frantic incon-
sequential gastronomic mystery of mysteries, life' (*Tulips and
Chimneys*, 145–147). The reader is moved to see in one of

Cummings' 'portraits' of a friend, the poet himself, one who 'out of spontaneous clumsy trivial acrobatic edgeless gesture of existence, continually whittles keen careful futile flowers' (*Tulips and Chimneys*, 138). Occasionally, as in his tribute to his father (*50 Poems*, 34) or to his mother (*Collected Poems*, 218), he gives us glimpses of himself that we wish were more often in evidence. This is likewise true in some of his 'Chansons Innocentes' in which he captures the sweetness and innocence of childhood. He achieves, too, a greater degree of simplicity than is his wont; but it is no Blake-like simplicity, although that would seem to be his aim.

Mr. Cummings' reaction to Picasso's work gives us a statement of qualities that strike a responsive chord in his own nature. Whether or not he is able to achieve in his own works the quality he most admires in Picasso is a problem we must later attempt to solve. He gladly turns from the 'gripping gigantic muscles of Cezanne's logic' to praise Picasso's mastery of 'form truly' in its greatest simplicity, form which the artist has created from Trees of Ego, lopped of every prettiness (*Tulips and Chimneys*, 102, 144; *Collected Poems*, 103).

Mr. Cummings is sensitive to nature in all of its manifestations. He can describe impressionistically the coming of dawn, of dusk, and of night; can capture the magic of a multi-coloured sky, of the wind and the waves; he can attempt to 'utter a tree,' or be aroused to ecstasy by a shooting star (*Tulips and Chimneys*, 91–101, 140–160). No season leaves him unaffected. His attitude toward 'most singular' spring differs from the usual attitude in that she is no neat goddess but the 'slattern of seasons' (*Collected Poems*, 280; *Tulips and Chimneys*, 129, 130); one might almost call her Botticelli's Primavera become riggish.

It is this riggish quality, in fact, that dominates much of his love poetry. In poem after poem Mr. Cummings reveals his sensitive and delicate idealism toward love; but he is afraid of this emotion, giving the reader the impression that he believes it to be unmasculine. He gives himself away, however, in his conscious attempts to reveal himself the strong, assertive male capable of looking at love realistically. The reader is constantly aware of the poet's going against his inner nature and desires. He forces himself to look at sex in all its frankness, but he cannot conceal the effect caused by such an expenditure of will. The result is that too many of his poems end by being surface treatments of love, and reveal all too clearly his essential immaturity. Many of his 'Amores' (*Tulips and Chimneys*, 66–82) convey a certain tremulous ecstasy, but it is not the ecstasy of a profoundly experienced emotion. They lack substance. To put it crassly, I at least receive the impression that Mr. Cummings is trying too hard to be poetical. In later poems, however, he does occasionally achieve a slight deepening of the tone, although he does not thoroughly convince me that it is an wholly adult one (*Tulips and Chimneys*, 18–20, 25; *Collected Poems*, 224, 225; *lxl*, xvi, xix, etc.).

Mr. Cummings is almost feminine in the manner in which he wishes to be absorbed in love and the untrammelled life of the senses—feminine or oriental. Many of his love poems are consciously modelled after the 'Song of Solomon' with their love of luxuriant imagery (*Tulips and Chimneys*, 'Orientales,' 52–56). 'Love's function,' the poet iterates again and again, 'is to fabricate unknownness.' Because this quality is so often apparent in his work, the reader need not be surprised to find it hard for the poet to face certain realities, an important one being the downright pleasure that a woman can find in the sexual act. He reluctantly grasps the truth, is revolted by it, and attempts to escape by associating with harlots, where he feels such an attitude to be acceptable. He finds it surprising that a society woman, reserved and dignified before the world, should be anything but frigid in bed; but he can force himself to accept the inmates of Dick Mid's house (*Tulips and Chimneys*, 'Realities,' XVIII–XX). He tries,

I think, to conquer his sense of revulsion by a sophomoric frankness. At one time he seems to strive for the effect achieved in the last chapter of *Ulysses*, but he achieves only a pornographic effect (*Tulips and Chimneys*, 143; *Collected Poems*, 262): at another he delights in the actual description of the sexual act (*Tulips and Chimneys*, 142).

The result of his reactions is that sex assumes a place in his poetry out of proportion to his ability to say anything new about it. The reader can appreciate those poems of awareness in the manner of some of those of D. H. Lawrence; he can accept poems that are frankly sensual and physical. But one theme too often repeated tires, and especially so if the treatment of the theme at forty-five differs in no apparent way from its treatment at twenty-five. The younger man may well think that through the physical he is awakened into a reality as important as that possible to the reaches of the mind. But to think of it as the only reality and the only thing worth while is certainly adolescent. I think it is Wells who somewhere said that equally important were work, thought, and ambition.

It would be incorrect to say that Cummings makes no allusion to these matters in his poetry. Unfortunately, however, his treatment of such matters reveals the paucity of his thought. It is not only that he hates humanity for its materialism, but he hates it for those things of which he himself is often guilty: its vulgar sentimentality and its absorption in sex. Aware that man's earthiness is in constant conflict with his spiritual achievements, he thinks of himself as a person apart. He attacks the bourgeois attitude towards life, unable to think of anything more distorting than so-called civilization. He derides the desire for security or for a conservative attitude towards life, but possesses none of the qualities of the true aristocrat that we find in poets like Shelley or Byron.

He is a snob who tries to feel superior the better to conceal his sense of inferiority (*Tulips and Chimneys*, 83, 115; *Collected Poems*, 123, 304–308; *50 Poems*, 28; *lxl*, ix, xii, xiv). Many of the 'realities' about which Cummings writes lack the ring of genuine poetry.   Often they are *tours de force* with no strong sense of sincerity, although, of course, there are exceptions (*Tulips and Chimneys*, 114).   Effective vignettes though they be, their limitation is their lack of magnitude.   Too often their aim is to shock; nothing more.   Whether it be a picture of a Cambridge landlady somewhat in the manner of Mr. Eliot's early work, of a madame of a house in New York or Paris, of the girls in general, or of Liz, Mame, Gert, May, Fran, and Kitty in particular, or a sordid picture of drunkenness during the prohibition era of Bill and his 'chippy,' or of Eddie and his 'broad,' the effect is the same.   He has confused realism with sordidness in the same way that a young student of sociology might mistake for the true reality the surface qualities he sees on his first visit to a slum.   The student has glimpsed a surface picture which is as far from the true reality as is an over-romanticized episode seen through rose-coloured glasses.   If poems of this type appeared only in *Tulips and Chimneys* the reader could excuse the poet on the grounds of his youth, but when they appear in *Collected Poems*, and *lxl* (1944), he loses patience, especially when at least thirty poems are of this nature.   He regrets the rarity of poems like 'the skinny voice' (*Collected Poems*, 98).

Mr. Cummings best displays a strong satirical sense in those poems in which he castigates man's general inhumanity and lack of sincerity.   He does not object to the way the average person licks the boots of success, but he heartily dislikes hypocrisy.   Whether it be a public speaker praising those fallen in war, the blind adoration of the devout before a funeral procession, the treatment of a conscientious objector, the hollow Christianity of the crowd, his outraged senses find expression in bitter satire.   At times this satire is trenchant (*Collected Poems*, 101, 147–151, 156, 163, 204); at times, arising as it seems to do from a smug superiority (*Collected Poems*, 244–248, 260, and others), it convinces the reader of the poet's outraged idealism.

What is the final effect on the poet of his contacts with the world? Earlier he is occasionally tempted to long for nothingness, particularly when, caught up in the beauty of the night in 'a connotation of infinity,' he realizes the smallness of man. Later, he looks more fixedly at what he has been duped into regarding as the realities of life.

Mr. Cummings' claim to a place among the important modern poets must rest, then, not on what he says, but upon his way of saying it—his technical achievements in extending the capabilities of poetry. It is not too early to attempt an evaluation of his technique because, as is now generally recognized by most of his readers, no important changes have occurred in his methods since his early work.

Although superficially a radical poet in his methods, his rhythms, instead of being in any sense original, are strongly traditional, and more in the manner of the Georgians than of any other. He possesses a sensitive and delicate ear. Many of the poems have a pleasant lilt, and are in themselves amusing, if slight. 'Red flag and pink-flag' (*50 Poems*, 11), for example, is in the rhythm of the nursery rhyme of 'Pease porridge hot.' I also sense an occasional influence of Edith Sitwell (*Collected Poems*, 211, 214, and others). His sonnets might seem to break from the traditional, but in fact do not, except in the most superficial manner. Because they have fourteen lines, he classes them as sonnets, and many do follow the English or Italian form, but many are irregular. But at no time does the reader sense a radical inner change such as is everywhere evident in those of Hopkins. Incidentally, some of Cummings' most successful poems are those which are unashamedly traditional, like the third in his 'Unrealities' (*Tulips and Chimneys*, 186). His poems in the oriental manner have an anachronistic flavour. He sometimes achieves a pleasant effect in the manner of 'counting-out' rhymes (*Tulips and Chimneys*, 26, 27, 29), but he becomes so absorbed in the technical aspects of his problem that he fails to inject the necessary passion. In one instance, at least, he attempts to treat his theme of the singularity of spring in the manner of a canon. At his worst, his verse assumes an undergraduate or jog-trot facility (*Tulips and Chimneys*, 22–24; *Collected Poems*, 201).

The innovations which have attracted most attention are essentially typographic and are of value only as they control the tempo at which the poems should be read (*Tulips and Chimneys*, 54, 142). For the most part I can see no real reason for the manner in which Mr. Cummings breaks up his poems. They lack form, by which I mean the careful integration of all the parts to compose the whole. I fail to be aware of the inner tension necessary for effective communication. No amount of clever manipulations of words, technical swagger, or innovation merely for the sake of innovation makes a poem. The following is an extreme example, perhaps, but what does it convey to the reader?

life hurl my
yes, crumbles hand (ful released conarefetti) ev eryflitter,
                                    inga where
mil (lions of aflichf) litter ing brightmillion of S hurl;
                                    edindodg: ing
Whom areEyes shy-dodge is bright cruMbshandful, quick-
                                    hurl edinwho
Is flittercrumbs, fluttercrimbs are floatfallin,g; allwhere:
a: crimbflitteringish is arefloatsis ingfallall! mil, shy mil-
                                    brightlions
my(hurl flicker handful
in) dodging are shybrigHteyes is crum bs(alll) if, ey Es
                                    Collected Poems, p. 145

'Bright millions' gains little by becoming milbrightlions,' nor

does 'hurled in dodging' when set up as 'hurl; edindodg: ing.'
Or take the case of old Mr. Lyman fresh from a funeral, ruddy
as the sunrise with blue true two eyes. What does the poet
hope to gain from setting it up in the following manner?

> old mr ly
> fresh from a fu
> ruddy as a sun
> with blue true two
>
> man
> neral
> rise
> eyes

lxl, xxvii

Can it be more than the hope to conceal the fact that he has
nothing to say? He reveals his extreme nihilism in his 'y is a
WELL KNOW ATHLETE'S BRIDE? (lullaby | & Z,'
'r-p-o-p-h-e-s-s-a-g-r,' 'mOOn Over Owns mOOn,' and
others (*Collected Poems*, 193, 269–277). Is he trying to hoax the
reader when he writes the vacuous 'or as our hand organ
bleats sweet nothings or a rancid hurdy-gurdy gurgling
thumps something' as

> ! o-ras-ourh-an-dorg-an ble-at-ssw-ee-t-noth
>   ings orarancidhurd
> ygurdygur glingth umpssomet hings (whi, le
>   sp,arrow, s wince?

Collected Poems, p. 284

Actually, of course, the subject and the presentation are on
the same level of emotional immaturity.

Mr. Cummings tries for further effects by deliberate mis-
spellings (*Collected Poems*, 245, 251, and others), by switching
letters in words in the manner of Spoonerisms: 'rish and foses'

for 'fish and roses' or 'helves surling' for 'selves hurling'
(*Collected Poems*, 192, 199), and others. By such tricks—and
they are only that—he removes his poetry from the great
tradition. Poetry must be capable of being read aloud; most
of his is not. His effects are as much visual as aural. He is not
concerned apparently with communicating his feelings about
ideas, but is trying to achieve in poetry what the abstractionist
achieves in art. It is the most attenuated aestheticism.

Fortunately for Mr. Cummings, however, he has revealed
in his less extreme experiments qualities of genuine poetry.
These qualities become most manifest in his images and that
phase of his diction in which he plays ducks and drakes with
traditional parts of speech. These two qualities coalesce.
He makes verbs out of nouns, nouns from adjectives in a
more decided degree than is customary. He is not innovating
here, as some may imagine, because this transposition of words
of one category to words of another is a characteristic of the
English language that has been in constant operation. It is
more frequent at some periods than at others and extremely
active at the present time.

When the poet writes, therefore, that 'if a look should april'
him (*lxl*, xl), he not only carries on a tradition, but he achieves
a beautiful effect. Several poems in *50 Poems* and *lxl* employ
this device. He makes a noun of 'yes' in 'Yes is a pleasant
country'; of the adverb 'soon' in 'These . . . are /built of soon
carved /of to be born of /be'; and of the conjunctions of 'if'
and 'but' in 'she stiffly struts her ifs and buts.' He speaks, too,
of the 'witchery of almostness' (*lxl*, xxxviii, xliv; *Collected
Poems*, 262; *Tulips and Chimneys*, 18–20).

Mr. Cummings is frequently felicitous in his compoundings,
such as 'mud-luscious' and 'puddle-wonderful,' which capture
a child's delight in mud and puddles, or his 'eyeswhichnever-
smile' (*Tulips and Chimneys*, 44, 45, 158, 159). He places great
reliance, too, on the epithets with which he heightens the

impact of his multiple-images. He combines metaphor and
personification in the following:

> when the minute moon
> is a remarkable splinter in the quick
> of twilight
>
> *   *   *
>
> or if sunset utters one
> unhurried muscled huge chromatic
> fist skilfully modelling silence
>> *Tulips and Chimneys*, p. 204

He speaks, too, of the 'convulsed orange inch of moon
perching on this silver minute of evening' (*Tulips and Chimneys*,
212); of the 'green meadow of timelessness' (*Collected Poems*,
229). He characterizes a friend as 'an orchid whose velocity
is sculptural' and, as I have already quoted, a 'being, out of
spontaneous clumsy trivial acrobatic edgeless gestures of
existence, continually whittles keen careful futile flowers'
(*Collected Poems*, 97). His early efforts, however, reveal all
the weakness of the early Keats and Shelley (*Tulips and
Chimneys*, 16, 17).

Mr. Cummings' diction leans heavily toward the polysyllabic and learned in his earlier work with a too obvious
use of alliteration (*Tulips and Chimneys*, 9–15, 189, etc.), a
tendency which he has curbed in the best of his later work.
He is aware of the effectiveness of vowel progressions as well
as the greater earthiness possible by the repetition of the same
vowel sounds (*Tulips and Chimneys*, 18–20, 189). He achieves,
too, a nice suspension in his verse by having a rhyme word a
transitional one, as 'smile' rhyming with 'while' (*Tulips and
Chimneys*, 'Puella Mea,' 33–43); or by the use of assonance
(*Collected Poems*, 143). He uses repetition on a larger scale
to communicate a sense of nervous bustle (*Tulips and Chimneys*,
136), or better to convey a setting (*50 Poems*, 41).

His use of parentheses, normal and inverted, of commas

placed at the beginning of a poem or in the middle of a word, of exclamation marks, colons, and semicolons, of rules-defying periods will arouse a nihilistic or anarchic reaction in his reader. Like his habit of running words together or tearing them asunder at will the purpose is essentially one of controlling the tempo. The trouble is not worth the effort, often doing no more than some of his other technical innova-tions—that is, concealing the paucity of what he has to say.

Had Mr. Cummings begun with some of the poems in *lxl* and developed from there, we could look forward more hopefully to work with survival possibilities. We should expect, however, that this new work would be in a more popular vein. There is a definite charm in the following:

> true lovers in each happening of their hearts
> live longer than all which and every who;
> despite what fear denies, what hope asserts,
> what falsest both disprove by proving true
> (all doubts, all certainties, as villains strive
> and heroes through the mere mind's poor pretend
> immortally occurs beyond the mind)
>
> such a forever is love's any now
> and her each here is such an everywhere,
> even more true would truest lovers grow
> if out of midnight dropped more suns than are
>
> (yes; and if time should ask into his was
> all shall, their eyes would never miss a yes)
>
> *lxl*, xxxvi

Charming, too, is the title-poem of *lxl*, charming in the manner of the lyrics, say, from *Annie Get Your Gun*:

> We're anything brighter than even the sun
> (we're everything greater
> than books

might mean)
we're everyanything more than believe
(with a spin
leap
alive we're alive
we're wonderful one times one

                                                      liv

But charm is not enough.

STEPHEN VINCENT BENÉT
(1898—1943)

FEW poets have enjoyed a more consistently favourable press or a greater immediate popularity than Stephen Vincent Benét, who died at the age of forty-five. Many persons already believe that he paid too great a price for the immediacy of his popularity. His shorter poems deal with love, God, death, and other imponderables, with the minutiae of life, with man as a social animal, particularly American man, and then often as a denizen of New York. Other American poets have written exclusively of Americans, as has Benét, but in the work of none is it so consciously stressed. They have written about it because it is the thing they know most intimately; he, not only because it was the thing his experience had given him, but because he was widely read in the formal and informal history of America from the earliest days to the present. He often gives the impression of trying to do for the America of his generation what Whitman did for his, or tried to do. Fully aware of the pitfalls awaiting him—

> Where the great huntsman failed, I set my sorry
> and mortal snare for your immortal quarry[1]—
> *John Brown's Body*, p. 3

he has attempted to see the relation of the parts to the whole with a story-teller's eye, not only of the past, but of the present. He has not only steeped himself in the stories of the earliest settlers and those of the Civil War, but he is equally aware of the callousness of to-day's public to a person of great spiritual beauty ('The General Public'), or of the ridiculousness of the idea underlying the usual bachelor dinner.

[1] Throughout this essay, except for *Western Star*, I have used the pagination of *Selected Works*, vol. 1, 1942.

However great the realization of the full scope of Benét's subject-matter, the careful reader never, except for a few all-too-rare moments, has the conviction that he has sufficiently assimilated or completely enough integrated his material to make it his own, without which there can be no incisive and compelling aesthetic impact. Particularly is this so if we remember that poetry is the most delicate and concentrated form of human emotion. Benét is not an impassioned man speaking to men of heightened sensibilities. He is the average man speaking to average men. His chief defect is a lack of inner tension, or of a disciplined muscularity. The thought has a surface brilliance, often more, but the prosody supporting it is insufficient to enable it to spring to life. The causes for this great deficiency are many, and we must examine them all, reserving for final analysis his two most ambitious works: *John Brown's Body* and *Western Star*. 'Complaint of Body, the Ass, Against his Rider, the Soul,' for example, has received high praise. The theme of this poem in irregular couplets is that of the soul's reaching out and the body's contentment with the physical comforts. It differs from most poems on this subject in its mood. It is, of course, not necessary to be long-faced about one's striving; but one must be aware of the striving. Unfortunately, the too facile rhythms communicate no sense of striving at all. The defects of 'Portrait of a Boy' and 'Music' are of a different nature. What might pass with some readers as verse is prose. Such lines, for example, as 'after the whipping he crawled into bed,' or, in spite of the rhyme, 'My friend went to the piano; spun the stool A little higher; left his pipe to cool' have no inner tension, no vibration, no density. The portrait has, nevertheless, a certain nostalgic charm because of its faithful presentation of a normal imaginative boy into which the reader injects his own experience. In much the same way, 'Portrait of a Baby' flushes in the reader sentiments similar to those experienced by the poet, and the poem therefore seems pleasant. A correspondence is created between author and reader; but it is not the poet's experience that is recreated through the medium of words. To a greater degree than usual, without his own experience to supply the gaps, the poem could not succeed. In the eight sonnets called 'The Golden Copse,' in which he speaks of his lost youth, one never senses the use of the inevitable word. The verse is not only pedestrian, but the images spring from no deep inner experience and, particuarly in the first, are strongly literary in their origin.

Although Benét has used a great number of verse forms, he is supreme in none. Too often he has been unwise in his choice of models. Instead of choosing those poets as models who have worked greatly in the traditional forms, altering them as they have hammered them into a shape suitable for their own needs, he has rather inclined to the lesser craftsmen of the nineteenth and twentieth centuries. I sense the influence of Masefield's seven-stress line in 'Expressions Near the End of Winter,' of Millay's 'Renascense' couplets in 'The Quality of Courage,' of Eliot's 'The Love Song of J. Alred Prufrock' in 'Operation,' and of other Eliot in 'Notes to be Left in a Cornerstone.' He becomes incredibly dull in his poem to Vachel Lindsay, 'Do you Remember, Springfield,' and in the poor imitation of Whitman's verse in 'Ode to Walt Whitman.' This last poem with its lack of inner tension is in sharp contrast to the quality in Whitman's verse arising from his intense vitality. Parts of *Western Star* bear a striking resemblance to the couplets in Amy Lowell's 'Evelyn Ray.' He dilutes what has already been diluted, just as he weakens the verse of Coleridge's 'Christabel' in the following passage from *John Brown's Body*:

> And slander is sinful and gossip wrong,
> But country memories are long,
> The Appleton clan is a worthy clan
> But we remember the dancing man.
>
> P. 39

One unconsciously compares 'Ode to the Austrian Socialists' with Spender's 'Vienna' with its much tighter rhythms and its deeper feeling. Benét's nearest approach to a prosodic innovation is probably his free unrhymed verse of 'Nightmare at Noon' and sections of *John Brown's Body* and *Western Star*. He attempts to tighten this rather structureless verse by the obvious use of repetition, but I do not think successfully. One frequently wonders whether in this he influenced MacLeish or MacLeish him.

Benét is often near his best in his light or ironic verse—as in 'For City Spring' in which the desire for cleverness rather than deep conviction leads him into a modification of the thirteenth-century 'Sumer is icumen in'—and in that for children, as in 'A Nonsense Song,' 'Evening and Morning,' 'Legend,' 'For All Blasphemers,' and so forth. The reader senses a sincerity he often misses in his more serious work.

He is at his best in his ballads such as that about William Sycamore. Here the obviousness of his images is not the defect that it elsewhere is. A more glaring defect is the unsubtlety of his strongly articulated rhythms. The ballads on American themes are decidedly better than those on foreign ones. 'Alexander the Sixth,' for example, is poor Browning; but 'Captain Kidd,' 'Thomas Jefferson,' 'John James Audubon,' and 'Western Wagons' possess a distinctive charm. So, too, do his poems on New York themes. His New York poems, in fact, are among his most original and best. 'Metropolitan Nightmare,' 'Notes to be Left in a Cornerstone,' and others in this group differ in quality from most of his work because he has adequately communicated in an imaginative and amusing form the integrity of immediate experience.

Before considering *John Brown's Body* and *Western Star*, the two major works of Benét on which his chances for survival will ultimately depend, one other much-praised work warrants a digression. 'Listen to the People' foreshadows the type of thing that has been brought to its ultimate folly by Norman

L

Corwin, and is similar to some of the radio scripts of Archibald MacLeish. The movement is a staccato, unrhymed irregular verse strongly end-stopped. Effective on the radio and making a strong appeal to easy thinkers, it is topical propaganda that may have historical but no poetic interest. It is difficult to understand how Benét could think he was catching contemporary speech-rhythms in this type of verse. He may have confused the speech-rhythms found in radio scripts with the genuine speech-rhythms of to-day. It is frightening to think of the power of this bastard pseudo-form on the general radio audience; especially when it is linked with the rankest form of chauvinism. From every aesthetic point of view it is meretricious; yet the response to it is tremendous, even from persons who should be more discriminating. It is trickery of the most obvious sort that from its very success beguiles the perpetrator into prostituting his talents.

But to return. As a medium for presenting to a popular audience a kaleidoscopic picture of the manifold diversity of elements in our war between the North and South and the earlier days of the settling of America, *John Brown's Body* and *Western Star* may always be valuable. They do in their way what James Boyd in *Drums* has more effectively done for our revolutionary period. It is possible that they will lead some of their readers to primary source-material. Although one never doubts that Benét has read widely in the formal as well as informal source-material, there is some doubt whether he has fused the diverse elements of his 'epic' into an aesthetic unity. He succeeds better in *Western Star* than in *John Brown's Body*, and for fairly obvious reasons. He does not overdo his use of the leit-motif to the extent that he does in the earlier work. In both, it is true, he adopts a different prosodic scheme for each group of characters; a four-stress anapestic couplet for Dickon Heron (*Western Star*) and the Wingates (*John Brown's Body*), regular blank verse for Sir Thomas Smith (*Western Star*) and Jack Ellyat (*John Brown's Body*), and so forth.

In music the use of the leit-motif can do much to control the auditor's emotional response. But even there it must be subtly handled in order to contribute to the sense of form, not to take away from it. The gradual manner in which the introduction can be made in music is impossible in poetry; impossible, that is, unless it is being handled by a master like Shakespeare or Milton. In *Samson Agonistes*, for example, the verse moves from a strongly masculine tone to one of seductive charm just before the appearance of Dalila. But in Benét there is none of this, nor an attempt at it. His abrupt transitions destroy the essential form of his work. The greater formlessness of *John Brown's Body* than that of *Western Star* arises from the greater frequency and greater abruptness of these transitions. Had Benét lived longer he might have solved his problem. I cannot conscientiously believe, however, that he would have done so. The goal which he had yet to reach was scarcely within his sight; not at all within his possibility of attainment. Let me illustrate. The prelude of *Western Star* is very free. Various rhyme-schemes and various stanza-patterns as well as echoes of popular songs, spirituals, and so forth, are in juxtaposition. It is all clear and all a little too facile. Book I begins with a five-stress unrhymed verse (not strictly blank verse), then shifts (22) to a four-stress anapestic couplet; at page 28 it returns to the five-stress, shifting a little later (the birth of Humility Lanyard) to what is little more than prose broken into a pattern; then at page 32 (Sir Thomas Smith) he changes to a regular blank-verse, the texture of which is immeasurably tighter than that of the other sections, although it is still not taut. He soon shifts again to the four-stress couplet and by so doing unpleasantly jolts the reader. He introduces other prosodic innovations at various points. In *John Brown's Body* the shifts are more frequent, more drastic, and more destructive of the possibility of sustained aesthetic impact. The reader who condones Benét's practice tacitly admits that he has denied himself the

exalting experience possible from a work of art the form of
which arises from the careful integration of the parts. In
painting it would be the integration of mass, line, colour; in
poetry of subject, diction, imagery, prosody, and architec-
tonics. On young persons from sixteen to nineteen not ripe
enough for a sustained work of any magnitude, both of these
long poems exert a powerful appeal. And one young man of
this age admitted to me that he dreamed of Sally Dupré for
nights. I am inclined to think, however, that Mr. Benét's
primary purpose was not such an appeal. Were the reader
conscious of any real reason behind the shifts, of any sense of
inevitability, he might feel different. But at no time is Benét
ever really muscular. The final effect is that of a newsreel
or a series of unrelated vignettes, not that of a complete
aesthetic experience.

Apart, however, from the too sudden transitions from one
facile prosodic form to another, other weaknesses exist.
These are the same that so frequently occur in the shorter
poems: infelicities of diction, slackness of texture, easy
images that do not bolster the thought, and the awkward
intrusions of the poet. The passage beginning 'Jack Ellyat,
least of any, expected attack' (107), for example, possesses a
staccato effect achieved by a succession of simple sentences
in the telegraphic manner of Hemingway's *The Sun Also Rises*.
Occasionally he interpolates a longer, rather highly figurative
passage, and then returns to the staccato style. Effective
though it occasionally is (not necessarily affective), it raises
the question as to whether or not it is poetry. A more obvious
example, however, is the passage about Sally Dupré (150–
170). This is mere journalistic verse, but it is not the poorest
in the work. For an example of this we need only turn to
the passage beginning 'so the deck is cleared and the host
goes back to its ships' (180). Benét has the further defect,
reflected in his diction, of being unable to get into his
characters, particularly those that are truly great. The Lincoln

soliloquy (186–196), which has somewhat the quality of a keening, is an apt illustration. And the description of the death of Jackson (245, 246) when read aloud reveals itself as prose. Of all the various sections of the poems, the best are unquestionably the ballads, those of Whistling Jack (205) and Sherman ('Sherman's buzzin' along to de sea,' 304) being the most outstanding. That he attempts to fit his verse to the subject is readily apparent in the six-stress line of 'Shake out the long line of verse like a lanyard of woven steel.' Unfortunately, the quality of woven steel is missing.

I have suggested that Benét's images do not bolster the subject. This, of course, is largely a subjective matter for every reader. I can do no more than suggest, therefore, what I consider to be weaknesses. One is inappropriateness. In his description of the soft-clouded night he mars the tone by speaking of the rats of night that had eaten the silver cheese, 'though here and there a forgotten crumb of old brightness Gleamed and was blotted' (40). The association of moon with cheese is unfortunate for several reasons, but the humorous childhood associations connected with it are alone enough to condemn it. Better is his characterization of Miss Louisa and Miss Amanda as 'proud dolls scissored from silver paper' (35), or of Elspeth Mackay's wit as 'a tartan of coloured weather' (20). Is he accurate, however, when he says that the 'warning beat at his mind like a bird and passed' (17)? He often makes a too obvious use of personification, such as that of October (14). It is the *easiness* of his images that accounts for some of his popularity. They give the non-poetry-reader the sense of reading poetry.

He also speaks of the skyscrapers lifting 'their foggy plumes of stranded smoke out of a stony mouth' (4), and of the effect of the differing sounds in America on the children of the homesick men whose wit would be 'whittled with a different sound' (4). Sometimes his images do not bear analysis. What does he mean, for example, when he says of the water that it was 'so cold it must be pure Beyond the purity of a dissolved star'? And does he not become unduly extravagant when he speaks of the prayers of women of the North for John Brown as

> Inexorably rising, till the dark
> Vault of midnight was so thronged and packed
> The wild geese could not arrow through the storm
> Of terrible, ascendant, women's prayers. . . .
>
> p. 44

In spite of many moderately good images, however, scattered through the poem, they contribute nothing to the ultimate form of the poem and are clever rather than inevitable, *montage* rather than part of the texture. I except one striking image from *Western Star*. He catches the very quality of the men on the ships when he speaks of them as 'cast grains of corn, The blown chance pollen, lost in the wilderness' (47).

At time Benét's style is downright spurious. His statement about Edward Brookes is a case in point:

> He had been alone when they landed, marched with the rest
> Now he lay dead all suddenly.
>
> *Western Star*, p. 48

The 'all suddenly' is inexcusable. He resorts to trickery, too, in the way in which he intrudes himself on the reader. He has been quoting Mr. Brua, one of Brown's prisoners:

> I like your way of talking, Mr. Brua,
> And if there still are people interested
> In cutting literary clothes for heroes
> They might do worse than mention your string-tie.
>
> p. 31

It approaches trickery, too, in the manner in which he makes the transition from what has been going on in the captain's mind in relation to sowing black seeds in American soil which sprout into 'a black-leaved tree . . . shaped like a yoke,' then shifting his figure to that of horses suggestive of the four horses of the apocalypse (12). He repeats the theme of the horses in Book I, 15, and again, only this time in a six-stress form, on page 23. Was his use of this to give form to the work? Or, if not actual trickery, the following is at least awkward: having mentioned several characters who had appeared earlier, he remarks,

> We have lost these creatures under a falling hammer.
> We must look for them now again.

I mentioned earlier that Benét was unable to get into his characters. This needs amplification. In searching the archives of American history he has taken the material that is the usual grist for the social-historian's mill and used it as material for his verse. He has looked at the divers elements that have played an important part in the shaping of America and has made them more readily available to his large reading public in a way that had only previously been sporadically done. And he has presented them in a pleasant way. I feel very strongly, however, that his acquaintance with his various types of character is literary rather than actual. A poet does not achieve realism in the manner attempted by the younger novelists writing between the two World Wars—by bald and earthy language. In a man of Benét's refinement, as I have also noted with Mr. MacLeish, there is a self-consciousness in his use of four-letter Anglo-Saxon words that over-empha-sizes them. They are as prominent and as unrelated to the structure as are the fungus-parasites on trees integral to the trees. Or if he knows proto-types of his characters, he knows them only superficially. His characterization arises from his rhythms rather than from psychological insight. In other words, he makes his verse do what empathy[1] should do and the result is two-dimensional. LaFarge's novel in verse, *Each to the Other*, suffers from the same weakness.

[1] See note on p. 30.

But if Benét is himsef not a poet, has he performed a valuable function for American poetry? From the point of view of technique his contribution is negative. He has carried on a tradition for which Whitman is largely responsible. At the time Whitman wrote, it was salutary both from the point of view of prosody and subject-matter. But it was not a style to be followed, and has been dangerous to those who followed it. Apart from style, however, Benét's manner of bringing divers elements of his story together is not a model for younger aspirants. His value lies in his selection of subject-matter. We must remember, as I have already suggested, that poetry is the most concentrated and delicate form of human utterance. If we remember this, we cannot grant Benét success as a poet. He realized that American themes need American and not English music, and sought, but did not find, the answer. He was fully aware that the task he had set himself of catching the manifold essence of America was a difficult and elusive one; and he believed that at the times when his imagination was at a high pitch of excitement he had succeeded. I do not think he did. Because of his use of American themes, he has been granted stature as a poet greater than he deserves. In some ways he has performed a disservice to American poetry by carrying on an already weakened tradition. If he has turned young poets to native subject-matter capable of being treated poetically, he has done something. He found his own best subject in New York City which he understood. In these poems we more nearly find the poet than anywhere else. It is only in these that he had the advantage of Jefferson Davis, who, he said, possessed

> All things except success, all honesty
> Except the ultimate honesty of the earth

p. 59

Only in these poems does he approach 'the ultimate honesty of the earth.'

HART CRANE

(1899—1932)

HART CRANE is a poet of a single short theme—the search for security. He weaves such divers and rich variations on this theme, however, that the inattentive reader easily loses sight of the basic melody. To the person who knows only the healthy atmosphere of parental harmony, economic security, and unobtrusive discipline, security (first manifested as love) is unawaredly a part of his heritage. He passes from childhood, through adolescence, to maturity without any sense of struggle or necessity for unusual adjustment. Reality holds no terrors. To a sensitive child, however, and Hart Crane was that, the lack of this security, forcing upon him as it did the necessity of shouldering 'the curse of sundered parentage,' the burden was too great. A well-rounded maturity was impossible. Crane's poetry lends support to the statement that a person's lacks are most visible in the light of what he most desires. Without biographical support—of which there is ample evidence in Philip Horton's excellent study—it reveals clearly enough the story of his blind, careening, chaotic endeavours to supplant the early insecurities.

It is too late for blame; and a critical essay is not the place for pity. One can only regret the immeasurable waste of talent by one of the most richly endowed of American poets. However lawless his personal life, as a poet he was a careful craftsman who fashioned his work slowly and meticulously, unseduced by the temptations of novelty and so-called 'new' movements. He was fully aware that the poet's concern must be, as it has ever been, 'self-discipline toward a formal integration of experience.' For poetry, he wrote, 'is an architectural art, based not on Evolution or the idea of progress,

but on the articulation of the contemporary human consciousness *sub specie aeternitatis*, and inclusive of all readjustments
incident to science and other shifting factors relative to that
consciousness.' He was not only aware of this; he practised it.
However misdirected, uncontrolled, nihilistic, or violent the
incidents in his life, when these are appropriated for a poem
they are handled with the objectivity of an artist seeking
significant form through the careful integration of all his
materials. His intense sensitivity as applied to the many facets
of life that came under his observation is largely responsible
for the richness of his work. It is futile and painful to ponder
what the results might have been had he been able to discipline
himself as he could discipline his materials.

Crane's poetry has often been criticized for its obscurity,
but real obscurity in his work is rare, rarer than in some other
poets not so considered. Such obscurities as there are arise
from compression rather than from confusion of thought.
A second or third reading resolves most of them; a knowledge of the biographical facts integral to the poem removes
all but a few. Most of the remaining, like 'Possessions' and
'Lachrymae Christi' are genuinely obscure because the poet
has attempted to express the inexpressible. Occasionally,
however, obscurity arises from his predilection for the 'musty
and brooding and esoteric.' He was himself aware of their
difficulty. The person who has experienced the esoteric mood
being communicated will recognize his successful communication; others will not. We must, then, regard these
poems as unsuccessful despite the excellency of imbedded
fragments.

The obscurities of compression arise largely from what
Crane called the 'dynamics of metaphor.' He was admittedly
often 'more interested in the so-called illogical impingements
of the connotations of words on the consciousness (and their
combinations and interplay in metaphor on this basis)' than
he was 'interested in the preservation of their logically rigid

significations at the cost of limiting [his] subject-matter and perceptions involved in the poem.' When he speaks of 'adagios of islands,' for example, the reference, to quote himself, 'is to the motion of a boat through islands clustered thickly, the rhythm of the motion, etc.'; when he speaks of 'nimble blue plateaus' the reference is to the speed and tense altitude of an aeroplane, 'implying the airplane and its speed against a contrast of stationary elevated earth.'

The obscurities arising from a failure to grasp the significance of a biographical reference are generally easier to resolve. The reader may justly accuse Crane of a failure in communication, but the richness of the poetry is so often increased by the suppression of certain details that he justifies his method. The full implications of

> In sapphire arenas of the hills
> I was promised an improved infancy

are only grasped by a knowledge of the family discord and separations. This is particularly true of 'The Broken Tower,' 'Havana Rose,' and parts of 'The Bridge.' The obscurity, however, is only that of a line or two and not of the whole poem.

Aware, then, of some of the difficulties and fully conscious that every complete poem has a richness and a fullness of meaning impossible to discern from the abstraction of its parts, it is important that we see his statement of the theme of insecurity. Since he is a person of intense feeling and of sharpened memory chronology is not strictly important, especially since so many of the poems are contemporary with 'The Bridge.' It is evident throughout his work that he derived a degree of sensuous ecstasy from his submergence in pain because from this has issued love and mercy. To have love (protecting him as it did from fear) and mercy were, he thought, worth any requisite suffering. This crying need for love was, of course, one aspect of his search for security;

another was a corollary—the feeling that he 'belonged.'
Denied this feeling because of the family dissension and
division, he sought it elsewhere, and often blindly. We must
remember, too, that he was an only child. In spite of fleeting
moments the sense of belonging eluded him. Rather, he
eluded it, because it was there, and only his own maladjust-
ment prevented his complete possession of it. The need for
this security and his attempt to resolve it either by self-
analysis or by positive assertion has led to his being called a
mystic. Rendered incapable by the maladjustments arising
from family discord ever to achieve security through the
normal channels of love, he sought it in homosexual contacts.
One disappointment led to another; soon the struggle ceased.
Eventually surrendering himself to the satisfaction of his
needs by the mere physical sensation, his unhappiness
gradually approached despair. The search for love and one-
ness is his major absorption in *White Buildings*, *The Bridge*, and
Key West.

A reason advanced for Crane's shortcomings as one
incapable of unified vision is that he did not know enough.
This implies that a formal education would have saved him.
It would have saved him, perhaps, had he accepted the
discipline this would have necessitated. It is impossible to say
that he would have achieved this merely by four years of
college. He read avidly and widely. He depended for his
vision on his feeling *before* the intellectual discipline, rather
than the feeling that emerges from the arduous intellectual
discipline, as in Dante, Milton, Goethe, and others. In order
to learn the secret of life's 'constant harmony', a necessary
step for anyone who would reach maturity, he resolved to
plunge himself into all experience. Only by the complete
submersion could he, he believed, win the 'bright logic.' In
his attempt to accomplish this, he made his great error—
albeit one common to adolescence. He mistook sensation for
experience, threw self-discipline to the winds, and, as a

result, found the going ever harder. Instead, therefore, of winning through to an emotional maturity, he remained always a tortured emotional adolescent. When, later, he did complete some of these early sensations into experiences, it was too late. He had so far weakened his moral fibre that he could not face reality. This is not to say, of course, that he was artistically immature. He was not.

His search for the unifying thread of life followed many paths; the absorption of self in the phenomena of nature, in love, and in the minutiae of daily life. But as I see it, his difficulty was his over-willingness to compromise, to be content with 'such random consolations as the wind deposits in slithered and too ample pockets.'[1] The mere fact that he attempted to sharpen his vision through the influence of liquor ('The Wine Menagerie' and his letters) is further example of this immature compromise. The vision that comes from a full look at the worst in utter sobriety is more accurate and less annihilating than one induced by artificial stimulants. It is unfortunate that Crane could not realize this or practise it. I believe, however, that he was fully aware that his own problem of orientation was the special case of the minority rather than of the general. He knew the danger to himself of too much fear and pity and that the world *was* 'dimensional for those untwisted by the love of things irreconcilable' ('For the Marriage of Faustus and Helen'), and he sought the unifying catalytic agent. He early seized upon the bridge as the symbol or myth, and he sought with 'all hours clapped dense into a single stride' to 'walk through time with equal pride.' Various facets of this idea find expression in 'For the Marriage of Faustus and Helen,' 'Voyages I, II, III, and VI,' and the idea itself is endemic to his major effort in 'The Bridge.'

Remembering that the several sections of 'The Bridge' were

---

[1] 'Emblems of Conduct,' 'Black Tambourine,' 'My Grandmother's Love Letters,' 'Garden Abstract,' 'Praise for an Urn,' 'Chaplinesque,' and 'Lachrymae Christi.'

not written in chronological order and that the actual poem covered a period of six years of composition, the note of insecurity is variously stated. In 'Atlantis,' the first section to be completed, he indulges in the strong rhetoric of affirmation, rather than the quiet statement of genuine conviction. The note is repeated in a Blake-like couplet from 'The Tunnel':

> Some day by heart you'll learn each famous sight
> And watch the curtain lift in hell's despite.

It is also evident in 'Quaker Hill' and 'Indiana,' two of the last sections composed in a mood of intense disappointment after he had lost faith in the poem and the possibility of its completion.

A better indication of this persisting sense of insecurity is the evidence afforded by the poems in *Key West* and the uncollected poems. Crane needed friends, and had them. But no one could have taxed his friendships more than he. Yet in spite of the loyalties of many, he could still write

> There is no breath of friends and no more shore
> Where gold has not been sold and conscience tinned.
>
> 'Key West'

At moments he seems to have found escape from the 'low evisceration' and to have achieved the longed-for unity. He had afternoons 'satin and vacant,' and could free himself from his baser nature—'the goat path . . . thence to tears and sleep'—and was bitterly aware, while fingering 'moidores of spent grace,' of what he had lost—'the bright stains that starred His throne.' Toward himself as toward the idiot boy, 'his trespass vision' shrank from facing his wrong. In lyric after lyric, he gives impassioned expression to his urgent need, but could neither find, nor if found, accept an offered solution.[1]

---

[1] 'O Carib Isle!' 'Island Quarry,' 'The Mermen,' 'The Idiot,' 'A Name for All,' 'Royal Palm,' 'The Hurricane,' 'The Broken Tower,' 'Old Song,' 'Enrich My Resignation,' 'The Sad Indian,' and others.

Crane was not unaware of the cause of his basic problem, but was already too unmanned to save himself. He took the immature attitude, however, of laying all the blame on others. After twelve years of submission to his emotions, it is tragic irony that he could still write that he must respect his emotions or he could not 'feel the necessary solidity to create anything worth while.' Never had anyone departed so far from the Platonic dictum to live by 'right reason,' or with more disastrous results. The pity is that Crane not only recognized his own state, although he would not face his problem, but he was fully aware that some men had succeeded in achieving the synthesis he sought. I think, in fact, he found a certain measure of security in knowing that they had. He admired Shakespeare's achievement ('To Shakespeare') and that of Dr. Zinsser[1] ('Havana Rose'), but the tragedy of his own inability to face reality, so evident in 'The Visible the Untrue' and 'Purgatorio,' finds final expression in 'A Postscript' and 'The Return.' Were the wren and the thrush his only final friends, or were they the ensigns of his faith 'toward something far, now farther than ever away'? With the consciousness of his utter failure, he returned to the bosom of the sea— 'me-her, into natal power . . .'

To appreciate the poetry in which this crying need for security is so universally imbedded will require from many readers a willing suspension of disbelief. Others will be too deeply moved by the pity and tragedy of Crane's personal life to approach the poetry objectively. Yet this is necessary. However chaotic was his life and lacking in integrity to himself as a man, as a poet he was a person of the utmost integrity and conscience. Although as time passed and the periods of

[1] Dr. Hans Zinsser (1878–1940), Professor of Bacteriology and Immunology at Harvard Medical School. World's leading authority on typhus. Isolated the typhus germ in 1936, and in 1939 announced the perfection of a method for producing enough anti-typhus to protect an entire nation. Books: *Rat's Life and History* (1937) and his autobiography *As I Remember Him* (1940), in which he accurately forecast the nature of his own death from cancer.

sterility became more and more extended his vision became clouded, we must not forget that the consciously stated theme of 'The Bridge,' as well as of many exquisite lyrics, was the search for the unifying thread in life, for such a vision as Dante achieved in his 'Paradiso,' but achieved after an arduous intellectual discipline rather than before, as Crane attempted to do.

Crane early realized that he could belong to no school, that it was legitimate for him to write something the way he liked to for his own pleasure. He had little sympathy for the despair school of the early twenties and took Mr. T. S. Eliot as a point of departure. Mr. Eliot's pessimism was all right for Eliot, but not for him whose goal, he said, was 'a more positive or . . . ecstatic goal,' and, he added significantly, 'I should not think of this if a kind of rhythm and ecstasy were not (at odd moments and rare!) a very real thing to me. I feel that Eliot ignores certain spiritual events and possibilities as real and powerful now as, say, in the time of Blake.' Crane's most absorbing problem was to give poetic form to the 'spiritual events and possibilities,' and it is his success in achieving form that will confuse the reader into thinking the limitations of his subject-matter less great than they actually were.

The problem of form became an increasingly more difficult one for Crane, as it does for every artist, with the growing consciousness that form must not be confused with mere outline. Only the major poets, as a rule, have been as keenly aware of the importance of the right word, the right image, the right rhythmic line, as was he. 'I am not at all satisfied with anything I have thus far done [he wrote], mere shadowings, and too slight to satisfy me. . . . One must be drenched in words, literally soaked with them to have the right ones form themselves into the proper patterns at the right moment.' This search for the words with which he could enrich the texture of his work led him along many paths, but it was in the Elizabethan dramatists that he, like Mr. Eliot, first found what he sought. He was anxious for words that would achieve the 'revelation' that he found in modern composers like D'Indy, Strauss, Ravel, Scriabin, and Bloch. To get what they did into words, one needed, he wrote, 'to *ransack* the vocabularies of Shakespeare, Jonson, Webster (for theirs were the richest) and add one scientific, street and counter, and psychological terms, etc.' Accustomed as the serious reader has become to the esotericism of many younger poets, Crane's vocabulary does not strike the reader as unusual. It is rather his unusual associations of these words for musical and emotional effect that bear his unique stamp. 'Bleeding eidolon,' 'borage of death,' 'thewed with levin,' 'pirouettes of a pliant cane,' and 'grimed tributaries' are random examples to which each reader will add his own findings.

The density or heavy-pile texture of Crane's lines is largely due, I think, to his methods of composition. The lines were hand-forged on the anvil of his brain. Lines originally created for one poem later find themselves transposed to another without alteration. He not only borrowed from himself, but he borrowed from others. The manner in which he borrowed and then subjected his borrowings to a series of reworkings until he had forged something very different from the original is well illustrated in Mr. Horton's 'The Greenberg Manuscript and Hart Crane's Poetry.' In 'Voyages II,' for example, Crane consciously borrowed phrases from four different poems, but the borrowings are not evident in the published version. Greenberg's line—'Silhouette set the sceptres roving'—appears first as 'enlisted by what sceptres roving wide from isle to isle,' then in the following variations: 'Silhouettes of sceptres roving,' 'set with sceptres roving,' 'circled by their sceptres roving,' 'shadowed sceptres roving.' At this point Crane introduced a new phrase of his own

M

making: 'in terror of her sessions.' In the final version, Greenberg's line is completely assimilated:

> The sceptred terror of whose sessions rends
> All else than Deity's green crested Herb.

A more difficult problem, yet one which he so successfully solved that his is a new voice in poetry and yet remains in the main traditional stream, was that of his rhythmic line. This line did not come without intense struggle and the assimilation of many influences. The beginnings in the fragment 'The Bridge of Estador' are certainly crude, but show a remarkable improvement in his free translations 'Locutions de Pierrot' under the strong influence of LaForgue. Crane hammered out his lines until they took the shape he wanted. Certainly they fall into no easy scansion, but if the reader recognizes the importance of paeons[1] in modern poetry, particularly the third ($\cup \cup / \cup$), he will have little difficulty. Except when the poet is being consciously and obviously free, the stresses are regular. The careful reworking and constant condensing to which he submitted his lines give them a texture as tight as those of Hopkins, a poet unknown to him in his early years of experimentation. They are rich with chained emotion.

His stanza-patterns are the most traditional aspect of his work, but only in one poem, 'An Old Song,' where he consciously strove for that effect, is the music of the pattern distinctly reminiscent of a former era. To his four- or five-stress quatrains, rhymed or unrhymed, he brings a new and subtle music. In parts of 'The Bridge' he captures the distinctive note of modern civilization. I do not know whether or not it was the result of Crane's experiments that influenced younger poets like Auden, Spender, and MacNeice to extend the range of these jazz rhythms and music-hall songs. He was certainly fully aware of what he was doing, and that in 'For

---

[1] Paeon: see note, p. 132.

the Marriage of Faustus and Helen' he had 'struck new *timbres* that suggest dozens more, all unique, yet poignant and expressive of our epoch.'

I do not mean to suggest that Crane was at all times successful. Too often, and particularly in such important sections of 'The Bridge' as 'Cape Hatteras' and 'Atlantis,' he has given us rhetoric instead of poetry. In 'Cape Hatteras' I think it was because of a failure in inspiration; in 'Atlantis' because of insufficiently crystallized vision. The third part of 'For the Marriage of Faustus and Helen' demanded more work than he was willing to give it. His greatest failures, however, were, I believe, because of his lack of ability to sustain an intellectual discipline.

Crane's images account for no small part of his worth as a poet. Many of these are readily grasped; others only emerge with several readings. These, the ones of course that arouse the enthusiasm of the reader, often make a particularly poignant impact when the biographical facts are known, as when he asks the Power to

> render my ghost
> Sieved upward, white and black along the air
> Until it meets the blue's comedian host.
> > 'O Carib Isle!'

Or in describing the sound of the bells before dawn, when the stars fade, he speaks of them as a swarm of bees—

> The stars are caught and hived in the sun's ray?
> > 'The Broken Tower'

Frequent mention has been made of the evocative quality of his similes. Well known is

> As silent as a mirror is believed
> Realities plunge in silence by
> > 'Legend'

He catches a delicate quality in Faustus' pleading with Helen, that symbol of absolute beauty:

> Imminent in his dream, none better knows
> The white wafer cheek of love, or offers words
> Lightly as moonlight on the eaves meets snow.
>
> 'For the Marriage of Faustus and Helen'

The almost Hopkins-like quality of these images plays an important part in regulating the tempo of the lines. They hold the reader to a contemplative pace.

Only the person who has had the opportunity to witness the glory of the shad, that lacy species of shrub-like tree, often confused with the dogwood, can appreciate the accuracy of the following:

> Cowslips and shad-blow, flaked like tethered foam
> Around bare teeth of stallions, bloomed that spring
>
> 'Cape Hatteras'

His fondness for music furnishes metaphors for his verbal magic. The wind, for example, mowed a sarabande on the mead ('Repose of Rivers') and spring blossoms are *'twanged red perfidies of spring'* ('Lachrymae Christi'). His use of 'chevron' as a verb in 'saw the first palm chevron the first lighted hill' ('Ave Maria') and his use of 'ruffles' in 'the fresh ruffles of the surf' ('Voyages I') are characteristic examples of his analogizing powers.

Crane's images reveal his complete absorption of the phenomena of modern America—its industrialism, its ugliness, and often its viciousness—as in the 'noon leaks, a rip-tooth of the sky's acetylene.' The moon can transform this ugliness into moments of beauty. He catches the mood of the moonlight on the windows of a deserted mill admirably in the following:

> Whitely while benzine
> Rinsings from the moon
> Dissolve all but the windows of the mills
>
> 'Lachrymae Christi'

His use of 'grail of laughter' in the following is right:

> but we have seen
> The moon in lonely alleys make
> A grail of laughter of an empty ash can
> > 'Chaplinesque'

His images also indicate the route of his disillusionment and suffering. Take, for example, those on memory. In one of his early poems while the idea of friendship and love is still roseate, he speaks tenderly of memory:

> Yet how much room for memory there is
> In the loose girdle of soft rain.
> > 'My Grandmother's Love Letters'

Later memory becomes a 'casual louse.'

Being an only child, friendships meant more to him than if he had brothers and sisters with whom he could have been close. But no one demanded more from and had less concern for his friends than he. Friendship becomes for him 'friendship agony' ('A Postscript'), and he later speaks of himself as one who with pledges, tastes 'the bright annoy of friendship's acid wine' ('Quaker Hill'). It is no matter for wonder, then, that a person who had suffered and given in to 'the steep encroachments' of his blood should arrive at the nadir of despair in an image that combines memory and friendship:

> The phonographs of hades in the brain
> Are tunnels that re-wind themselves, and love
> A burnt match skating in a urinal.
> > 'The Tunnel'

With a poet who is so wholly dependent for his subject-matter on his emotions arising from personal incidents, the full force of his images can only be grasped with a knowledge of the biographical facts.

In the fusion of his materials into significant form Crane was particularly successful in his short lyrics. 'Praise for an Urn,'

'Voyages,' 'Garden Abstract,' 'The Broken Tower,' and others amply attest this fact. He was incapable, however, of significant form on a larger scale. The first two sections of 'For the Marriage of Faustus and Helen' are more successful than the third. Whether it was the less amount of time spent on the third section or because the material proved more intractable, this third section is not sufficiently fused into the other two. 'The Bridge,' although magnificent in some of its parts, is not successful as a whole. The limitations of his powers result, I think, from his too great dependence on his own immediate emotional experiences rather than on the greater understanding and architectural strength resulting from a strongly disciplined intellect. A person not so trained is incapable of grasping the sustained ecstasy possible from this discipline. He lacked the stamina for sustained effort over long periods. Certainly his emotional exhaustion could have been more readily overcome had he not weakened himself by strenuous dissipation and violent outbursts.

Inasmuch as 'The Bridge' is his major poem, some analysis of it and of the poet's methods are necessary. Crane realized from the beginning that he had set for himself a difficult task. The 'channel forms' or mould had to be such into which he could throw himself at 'white heat'—a significant phrase—and he conceived the form as symphonic. He aimed at 'a mystical synthesis of America' and felt that 'history and fact, location, etc., all [had] to be transfigured into abstract form that would almost function independently of its subject-matter.' He looked upon the bridge toward which the initial impulses of the people would have to be gathered toward a climax as a 'symbol of our constructive future, our unique identity, in which is also included our scientific hopes and achievements of the future.'

This was in 1924. He began composition on the last section immediately. By July, 1925, he had a version very different from the first. Then he abandoned composition for two years. It was constantly in his mind, however, and we must not underestimate the importance of this period of contemplation and gestation on the final outline. Many incidents of his daily life—his friendship with a taxi-driver and Aunt Sally to mention two slight ones—were providing materials for the poem. Early in 1926, however, he had one of his recurring fits of depression and began to doubt the validity of his materials—emotionally he wanted to write it, but 'intellectually judged the whole theme and project' seemed 'more and more absurd.' By July his spirits had risen and within the next two months he finished the final version of 'Proem,' the greater part of 'Ave Maria,' 'The Tunnel,' revised 'Atlantis,' wrote 'The Dance' and 'Cutty Sark.' Then for two years he did little more except revise. When he once more began to write, he finished 'Harbor Dawn,' 'Van Winkle,' 'The River.' This left him 'Cape Hatteras,' 'The Cyder Cask,' 'The Calgary Express,' and '1927 Whistles.' These last three were never finished, probably not even begun. He finished the poem in October, 1929, with the writing of 'Cape Hatteras,' 'Quaker Hill,' and 'Indiana,' in 'a rage of disappointment.' It is evident from the mood of 'Quaker Hill' and 'Indiana' that he had lost his vision. Had he not earlier expressed his hope in 'Atlantis' the end could never have been written. Because of the method of composition and the change from hope to deep despair the final section strikes a false note in the poem.

Crane meant each section to stand alone and yet be integral to the whole. He fails in his integration. Not only is the bridge as a symbol not great enough to carry what he attempts to put into the poem, but many of the sections fail in their communication. They are obscure in their larger significance without a prose commentary. With a prose commentary such as he has provided in his letter to Otto Kahn and to various friends much of the poem is unconvincing. He fails to achieve his desired goal. 'The Proem: To Brooklyn

Bridge' is excellent. Neither of the first two sections—'Ave Maria' or 'Powhatan's Daughter'—quite comes off in spite of the high excellence of extended sections of the first and of the separate sections of the second. The difficulty of the first is his inability to express the large conception at which he aimed, and of the second the strength of the symbol. Without being told, I do not think the separate sections make clear the love-motif being carried along as 'a symbolism of the life and ages of man'—specifically, childhood ('Van Winkle'), youth ('The River'), manhood ('The Dance'), and age ('Indiana'). 'Harbor Dawn,' 'The River,' 'The Dance,' and 'Indiana' are excellent in themselves. Prosodically 'Cutty Sark' is technically exciting. Here, again, however, I feel he fails to make his symbol clear or its relation to the rest of the poem. 'Cape Hatteras' begins well, contains an interesting prosodic section capturing the fall of the plane, but degenerates into pure rhetoric. It communicates a sense of effort and strain. 'National Winter Garden,' 'Quaker Hill,' and 'The Tunnel' best reveal Crane's treatment of the contemporary material particularly as it has impinged upon his own personal life. It is the deeply personal note that gives them much of their value. The final section 'Atlantis' is in the nature of a rhapsode wherein he expresses his spirit of affirmation. The symbol was not great enough for the purpose for which Crane chose to use it.

In spite of the fact that 'The Bridge' is a failure, it remains a poem that deserves to be read many times if for no other reason than the sheer aesthetic pleasure its parts afford. In the final analysis that is the way in which all his poetry must be read. All good poetry must be able to be read in this way. The best poetry generally affords an ethical pleasure too. By ethical, I decidedly do not mean didactic. Any ethical satisfaction derived from Crane's poetry, however, must be essentially negative and in the nature of a warning of what not to do. In this, although in a different way, the effect is similar to that of much Jacobean drama where the reader senses the terrible effects of spiritual barrenness. Unfortunately the American poets who can give both an aesthetic and ethical satisfaction have been all too few. Limited as the scope of Crane's work therefore is, he must be recognized as one of the very few who, having made a distinct contribution to our heritage, merit survival. It is useless to lament his early suicide. The course of his life was such that he had given all that he could ever hope to give. He was not intellectual enough for any sustained work, nor was he able to treat a subject that was not essentially a personal one arising from his own gregarious contacts. He may have laid claim to vision, but he could not understand the full implications of the word. When he confined himself to a subject within his scope he gave us some of the finest lyrics we have yet had from an American.

EPILOGUE

THE foregoing essays are evidence that the present is not a great age for American poetry; nor in the light of the disruptive movements of the past four decades could we expect conditions to be otherwise. Ours has been essentially a period of experimentation, expansion, adjustment, and re-orientation to the great tradition of poetry. Although the general level of writing has been higher than at any period of our history, and although several poets have written one or a few poems that will enrich our heritage, we have only one poet who, in my opinion, has sustained a quality of poetic achievement higher than that of any previous American poet. That is Mr. Frost. He alone, I believe, will be assured a permanent place as a major poet in our literature. It is significant that England recognized his distinct contribution earlier than did the United States. Mr. Frost so quietly represented the best that is in us that we failed to recognize ourselves in the mirror he held up to us.

The question may arise as to whether we have any younger poets whose work merits watching. It is still too early, of course, for definitive statement about any of the younger poets whose first volumes have appeared in the present decade. Several have already turned to prose or abandoned literature altogether for more remunerative fields. In America, as elsewhere, the poet without independent means cannot devote himself exclusively to literature. Four poets have emerged that merit careful watching—Karl Shapiro (1913–), Randall Jarrell (1914–), Robert Lowell (1917–), and Robert Horan (1922–). The first volume of the youngest is pre-eminent in its promise.

From the point of view of technique, Mr. Shapiro is the most strongly traditional, although all show the marked influences of Mr. Eliot and Mr. Auden, and occasionally those of Mr. Wallace Stevens and Gerard Manly Hopkins. Mr. Jarrell, on the other hand, rather obviously discontented with rhythms at hand, sought to find new ones and to create a new medium. Neither Mr. Shapiro nor Mr. Jarrell, however, was wholly successful. Mr. Shapiro failed to imprint his own personality on his borrowed forms, and although he achieved extensive popularity, he failed to enhance his poetic stature. He has realized his danger and has attempted to avoid it in his latest volume, *Trial of a Poet*. Here he has concentrated his expression, and in such poems as 'We waged a war within a war,' 'The atheist bride is dressed in blue,' 'Homecoming,' 'Demobilization,' and 'Boy-Man,' he has found the right dress for his satirical ideas. His thought and emotion are here in equilibrium.

Mr. Jarrell's first volumes—*Blood for a Stranger* and *Little Friend, Little Friend*—gave the impression of tentativeness. The contemporary speech-rhythms which he sought to capture were brought under only partial control. His third volume, *Losses*, is interesting in that when he turned to traditional forms, the tentativeness disappeared and the forms themselves became unique.

Mr. Lowell and Mr. Horan have been moved by a deeper impulse and have altered the tradition from within. The reader feels in their lines a stronger sense of necessity than in those of the elder two. Mr. Lowell's poems are generally polished and clear, albeit with a sometimes deceptive clarity, and Mr. Horan's often have a fluidity and length of rhythmic line that is the desideratum of many modern composers.

One possible reason for the greater impact of the poems of the latter two over those of the former is that Mr. Lowell and Mr. Horan have from the outset possessed greater sensitivity for the inevitable word. Mr. Jarrell has shown a development of this sensitivity in such of his later poems as 'A Camp in the Prussian Forest,' 'A Field Hospital,' and

'Jews at Haifa,' but even the later poems of Mr. Shapiro show no such development. In spite of a discriminating observation, his communication too frequently lacks significance. His critical and satiric powers, greater than his poetic, suggest that he is writing from the head rather than from a heart controlled by the head. He needs to subject himself to the discipline of hard writing. He should absent himself awhile from the felicity of uncritical reviews which, perhaps, have clouded his objectivity toward his technical achievement.

None of the four makes the mistake of avoiding the common word. Mr. Lowell and Mr. Horan, however, achieve a greater plasticity with these common words in combination, and they have a more unerring sense as to when a rococo word better suits their purpose. They achieve a richer evocation, therefore, by a greater density. This is most evident in their images, single as well as extended. Mr. Lowell, for example, speaks of the children who see their fathers as 'colourless as seaweed on the floats At anchor off New Bedford,' and of the girls 'whose eyelids burn with brandy.' He catches, too, the sense of growing terror in his image of fear, the yellow chirper, beaking his cage; or the effect of mobilization for war in

> The war-god's bronzed and empty forehead forms
> Anonymous machinery from raw men.
>> 'Christmas Eve Under Hooker's Statue'

The following selection from 'The First Sunday in Lent, I' gives a better illustration of Mr. Lowell's qualities, with an echo of Hopkins in his placing of 'tingle':

> Lord, from the lust and dust thy will destroys
> Raise an unblemished Adam who will see
> The limbs of the tormented chestnut tree
> Tingle, and hear the March-winds lift and cry:
> 'The Lord of Hosts will overshadow us.'

More effective is the following from Mr. Horan's 'Soft Swimmer, Winter Swan':

> A last, a light, and caught in the air-ladder lark,
> south-driven, climbing the indian, swift dark and listen!
> Sped by the building cold and rare in ether, birds hasten
> the heart already taxed with cloud and cherubim—
> fretted heaven, strained songless and flown dim.

Mr. Horan shows a greater predilection than the others for the use of symbols to convey the atmosphere in which his spiritual being moves. He is never abstruse. Although he uses them, as does Mr. Eliot, to convey spiritual richness and dryness, his most extensive use of them is to describe the emergence of youth into complete manhood, and his growing awareness that the new state is starker than that of youth and heavier with responsibilities.

This awareness, and its attendant willingness to face the greater reality, is a quality of these four young poets. Both Mr. Shapiro and Mr. Jarrell communicate the sense of satisfactory adjustment to their environment. Each matured greatly as the result of his war experiences, and each has made a unique use of these experiences as the basis of his poems. Each possesses, too, a strong objectivity, Mr. Shapiro through his sharp satirical sense and Mr. Jarrell through a heightened compassion and pity. Of the four, Mr. Lowell chose the most difficult route—that of the conscientious objector. Readers will agree or disagree with Mr. Lowell's choice of routes according to their ages and temperaments, but no one can fail to be conscious of Mr. Lowell's personal struggle. Although steeped in the Puritan tradition of New England, he failed to receive from it the spiritual sustenance he so deeply craved. He also saw that it had failed the New England people. Disillusioned with his religion and with the populace, he sought consolation in the Catholic Church. Much of his poetry reflects his struggle for peace. Other New England poets have been as aware as Mr. Lowell of the effects of a dessicated Puritanism. Edward Arlington Robinson crystallized this tradition in his sonnet 'New England,' and Amy Lowell in 'Lilacs.' Mr. Frost in some of the North of Boston poems has commented upon it directly as well as by suggestion.

As a literary critic, my own quarrel with those who have gone Mr. Lowell's way is that it is the way of least resistance and their poetry suffers accordingly. I cannot believe that the beatific vision can thus be attained. It would be better to struggle to recover those values that Puritanism in the finest sense stood for in the seventeenth century. These, I feel, Mr. Frost has captured. It is natural for the idealist to decry the lack of spirituality in the populace, but his immaturity prevents his recognizing that it has always been so. The struggle to overcome it is the important thing. We must realize, however, that it is futile to waste our strength on those 'degenerate by themselves enslaved.' I think Mr. Horan realizes this, just as he is aware that the life of the imagination is not alone sufficient. Only as man makes his adjustment as political entity can he achieve true freedom. It will be interesting in his poems to come to watch Mr. Horan's communication of this broadened knowledge. Since a leavening process is at work in man's political thinking and since the rabid spirit of technical experimentation has subsided, the time is ripe for poetry to reassert the educative function that it surrendered in the nineteenth century.